Pretty Pretorialicious:

A photographic book

Tendai Rinos Mwanaka

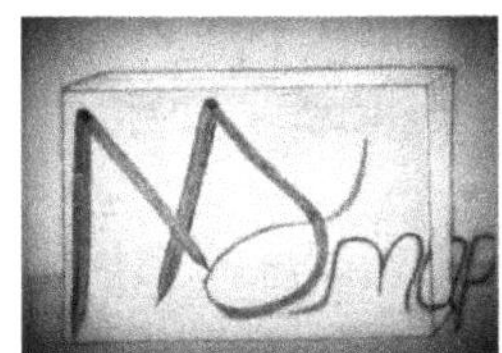

Mwanaka Media and Publishing Pvt Ltd,
Chitungwiza Zimbabwe
*

Creativity, Wisdom and Beauty

Publisher: *Mmap*
Mwanaka Media and Publishing Pvt Ltd
24 Svosve Road, Zengeza 1
Chitungwiza Zimbabwe
mwanaka@yahoo.com
mwanaka13@gmail.com
www.africanbookscollective.com/publishers/mwanaka-media-and-publishing
https://facebook.com/MwanakaMediaAndPublishing/

Distributed in and outside N. America by African Books Collective
orders@africanbookscollective.com
www.africanbookscollective.com

ISBN: 978-1-77934-040-5
EAN: 9781779340405

Table of Contents

Temples of our hearts
Bosman Avenue
Lining in
Watch out!
Water crisis
The Lion's bridge
Master of the Concrete Jungle
Francis Baad Street
Angular
Pull lines
No way in
Contained
Chessboard
Walking the Lillian Ngoyi way
Big Rex leftovers
Catholic Cathedral frescoes
Open exhibition: Food and Art
Street exhibition: human noises
Four four two
Arty, hanging…
Parked
Ndebele colours
State theatre
National Museum of Natural History
National natural museum dinosaur
Main entry into Burgers Park
Park dreams
Burgers park
The Big shade
Open Cave
Inside the Cave
House
Circular Church Square
Standing under our Gods

Square dreams
Way out
Sharing the park
Pigeons of Pretoria
Plumage
Guardian Angels
Hustling
Having a drink
Fish fish
Cityview 1
Welcome to my city
Cityview 2
Cityview 3
Cityview 4
Cityview 5
Cityview 6
Cityview 7
Mmap Multi-disciplinary Series

INTRODUCTION

I have lived in Pretoria for almost 3 years and in two phases. Unfortunately I lost most photos of my first phase of staying in this city, in 2017-2019, save for a few photos. I have included two of these photos to create contrast with the main thrust of this body of work, which I took in 2022, when I stayed in Pretoria from late December 2021 to early April 2022. In the two years I was out of Pretoria, I came back to see a lot of changes, especially depicted by the photos of statues, Krueger and Pretorius statues, at Church square and City Hall respectively. During the protests *Rhodes Must Fall* and the follow up *Fees Must Fall*, statues of colonial and apartheid figures were targeted and defaced or broken down so the government decided to fence these off.

This becomes the leitmotiv of this collection of photographs, the ongoing battle between the former rulers and present rulers, black and white, past and present, for space on Pretoria's arteries and veins, and as well in the minds of the people of South Africa. And on a deeper level the interrogation, and assigning of blame in the critical and sometimes constructivist memories and imaginations of the citizens of this country. As an outsider looking inside, I tried to show the battle lines in these photos. Pretoria space is a contested field between the past and present, and most of the inner spaces of the CBD are still hanging to the past. The disquieting feeling was whilst I counted about 3 former colonial presidents of South Africa statues (Krueger, Pretorius and Burgers) in the city centre there was only the imposing Mandela's statue at Union Building (which even at that is in Acardia) to remind the viewer they are now new rulers in this city and country. Maybe that's why Madiba's statue is monstrous and imposing? I have tried to organise my photos into groups, each is a character in this story, telling their own stories, that could be conjoined to the previous ones or yet to come photos, is this collection. The photos highlight the forming of Pretoria (City hall and Pretorius statues), the formation of the state of South Africa (Krueger statue, Union Buildings), the wars the people of South Africa were involved in (first and second world war) and dedications to their soldiers who gave up their lives defending humanity in further fields. One can't help notice there is nothing about Anglo-Boer war, and the struggle of independence in the city centre, of course these are at Voetrekker museum and Freedom Park, and both face off each other, just outside the CBD.

Then we have photos dealing with the architecture of Pretoria, from its browns beginning Dutch colours to British grey colours to the glass colours of the 21st century, I was mostly interested in the architectural angles of the buildings and roads, creating architectural music. And then there are photos of the picaresque streets of Pretoria, and I was more interested in the lines, the way that join plot to plot to create form. And then there are photos of street art, inclusive of drawings, paintings, sculptures and installations and I also highlighted two popular art spaces in the city, the National Natural Museum and the State Theatre. Because its street art, there is no way to separate it from the street and people, where we see in one of the photos, food and art is combined. This makes art accessible to humans.

The other collection of the photos is on parks, and I focussed on 3 parks, Burgers Park, Church Square and Union Building Park. Pretoria is a city with many parks, where its citizens utilises these spaces to meet and collaborate. I have always been fascinated by park spaces, and park benches. I would love to understand what of our lives we leave in these parks, so I am interested in taking pics of people sitting on park benches, or sleeping off and wonder what might be going on in their brains. Any good city should have these spaces, spaces to breathe, spaces to communicate with the green souls, spaces to imagine...

And another batch of photos takes a perspective view of the city, showing how Pretoria nestles among mountains, sprawling east-west, north-south, the way the concrete colours negotiate for space in this valley with the containing mountains around the city rendering the city an arching beauty. And on another deeper level, or surface level, as my title alludes, I was also interested in showing how sumptuous Pretoria is to the eyes, a city of beautiful buildings, clean streets, colourful streets, vibrant young humans and energies ....

Future work

I would like to continue photographing Africa's capital cities, showing how the politics of the countries are playing out and the beauties that these cities endows

Exhibition requirements

I would also like to have these pictures printed in A2 and or bigger sizes, framed and be exhibited in galleries and sold in limited edition runs

Rejoinder

When I compiled this book end of 2022, I hadn't thought beyond this contestation of space in inner Pretoria, and hadn't foretold what it portended, but the last general election in South Africa made me realise it is a real fight for belonging. No party managed to get majority votes and now they are being forced to actually share governance. There is a strong feeling of betrayal from the black people by both their black rulers (ANC) and White capital, seeing that the independence they had fought for hadn't stayed and ushered them into spaces they were blocked from accessing during apartheid.

HISTORY

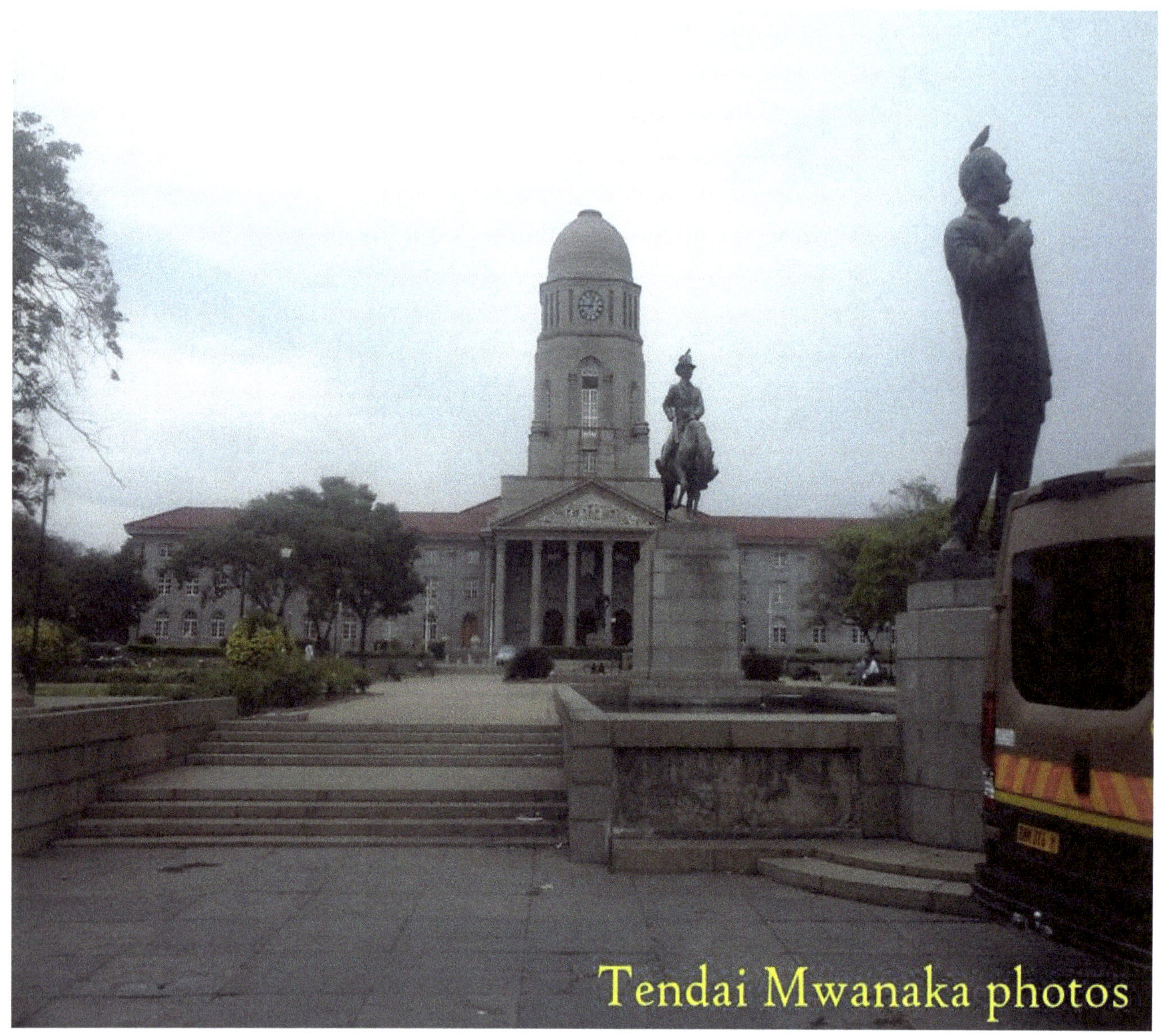

Pretorius statue before "Rhodes Must Fall" protests
2018

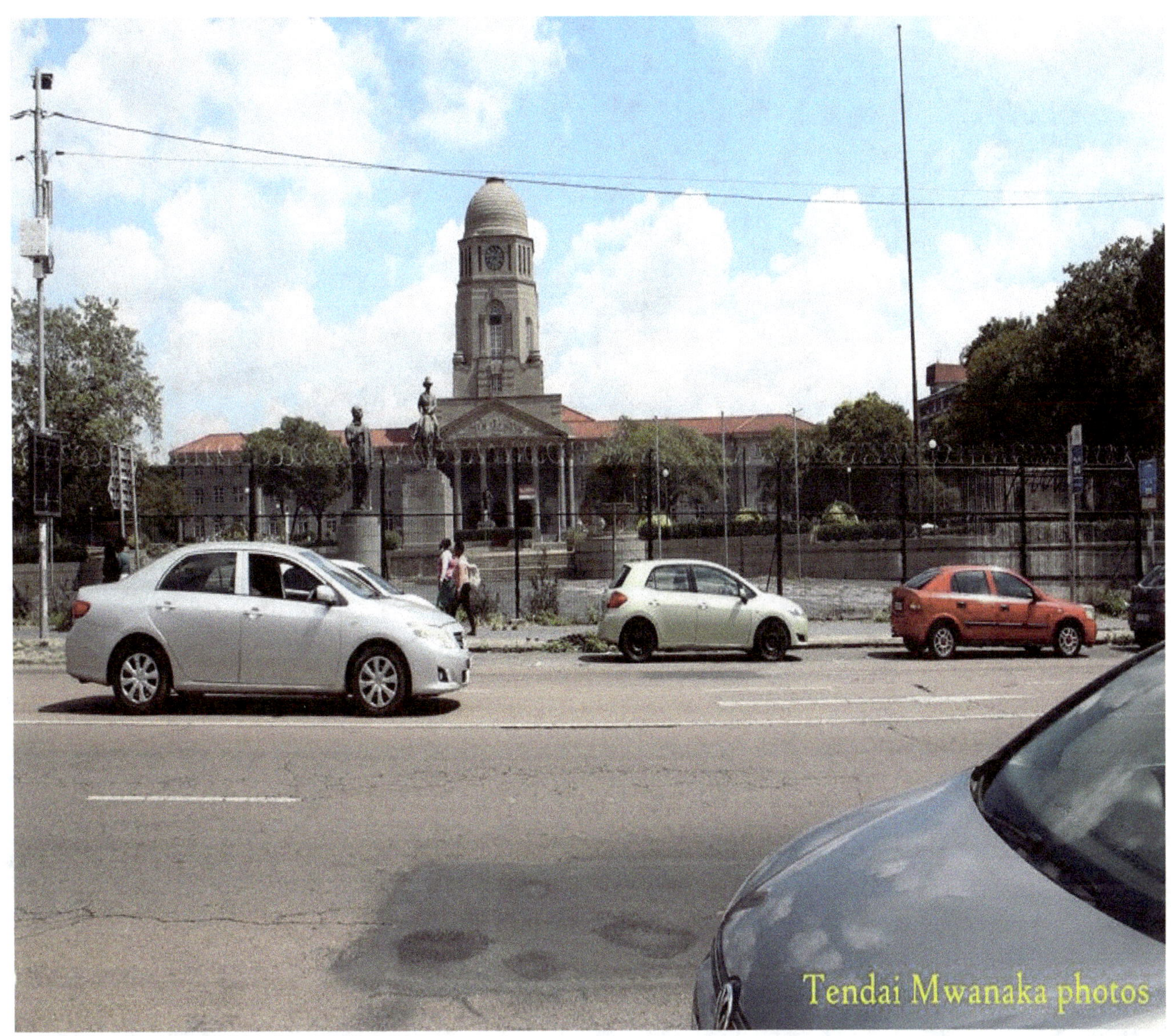

Fenced off Pretorius Statue after "Rhodes Must Fall" protests
2022

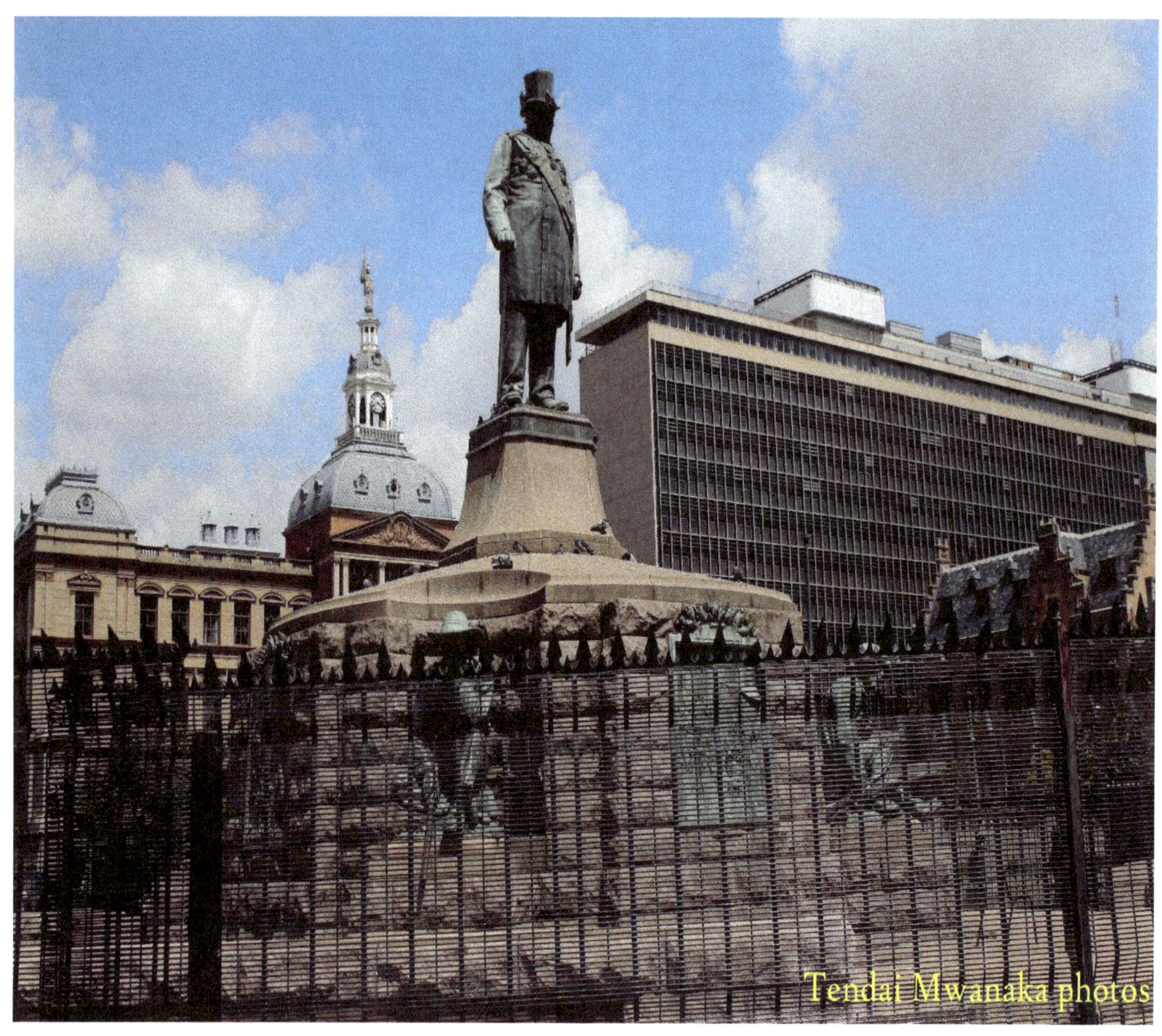

Fenced off Krueger statue
2022

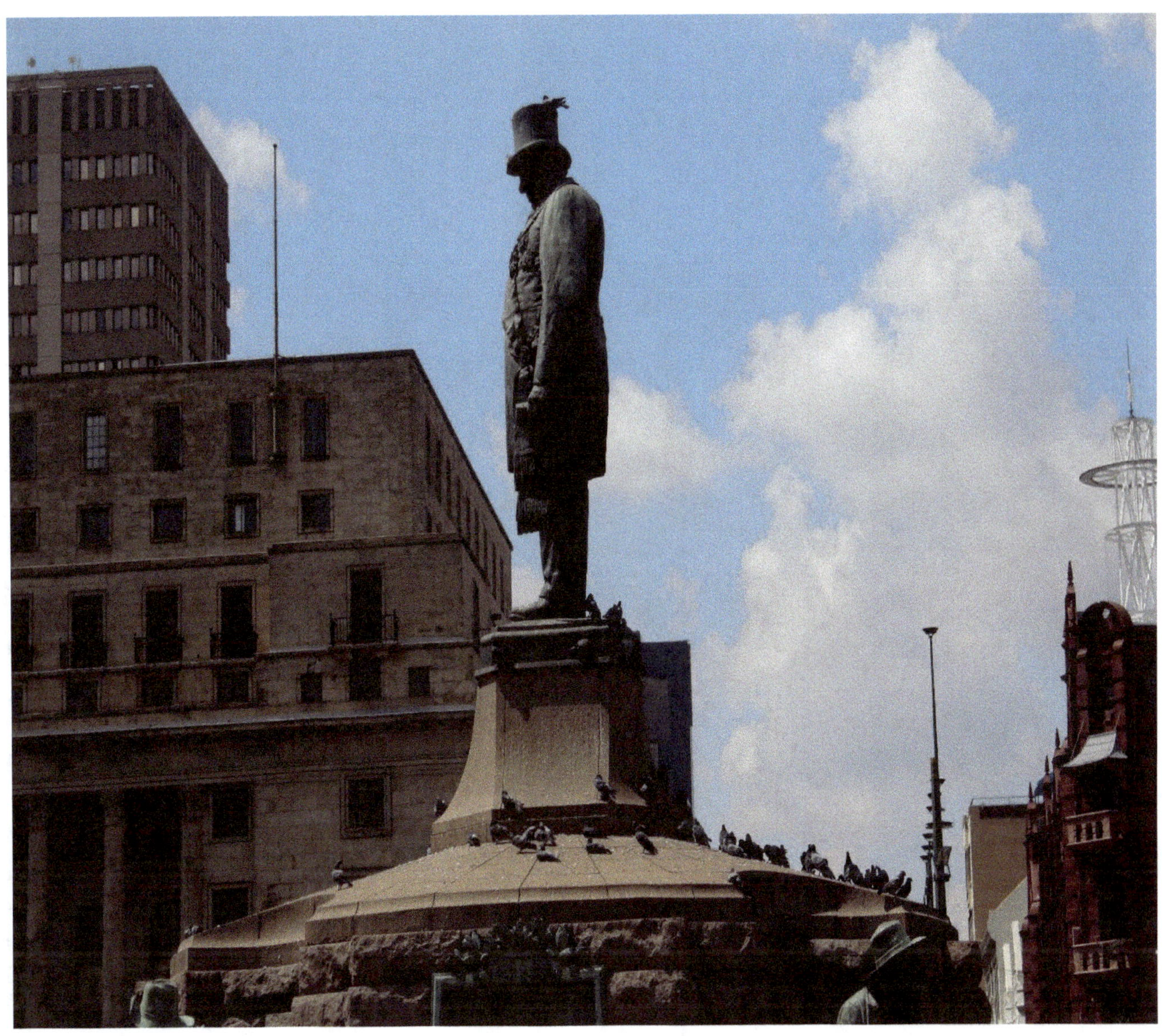

Krueger and his birds
2022

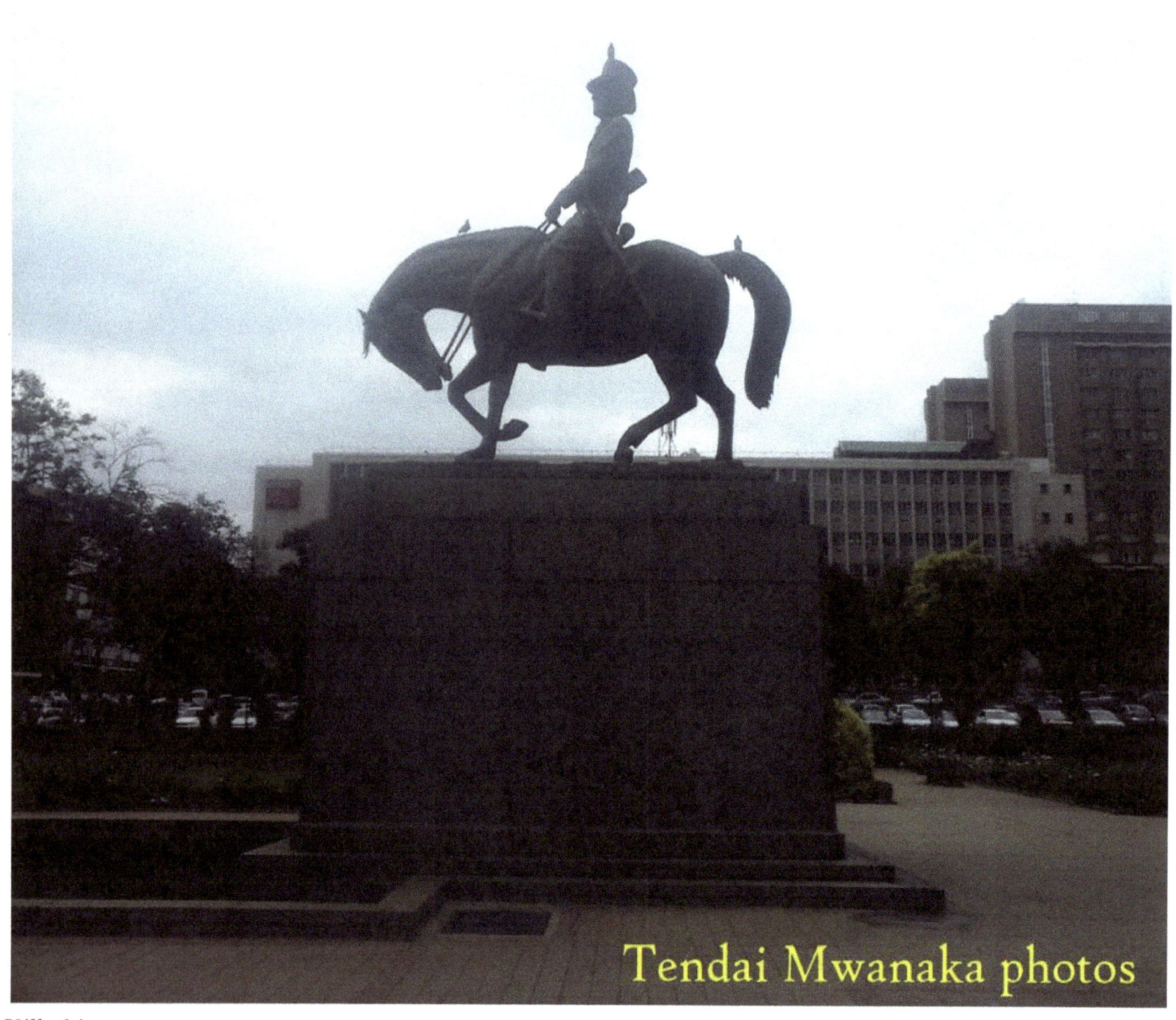

Killed in a war
2018

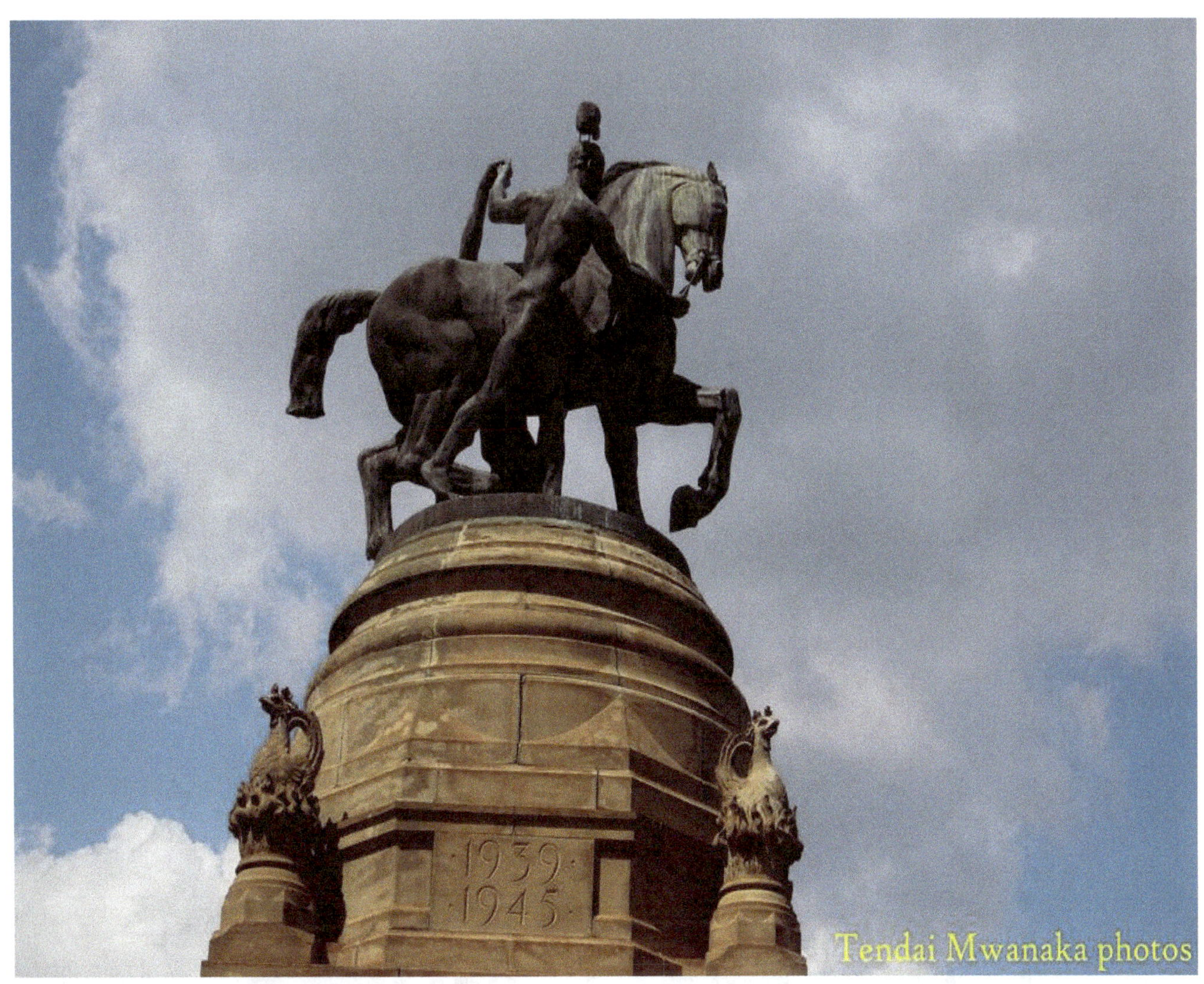

Fallen soldiers in the Second World War
2022

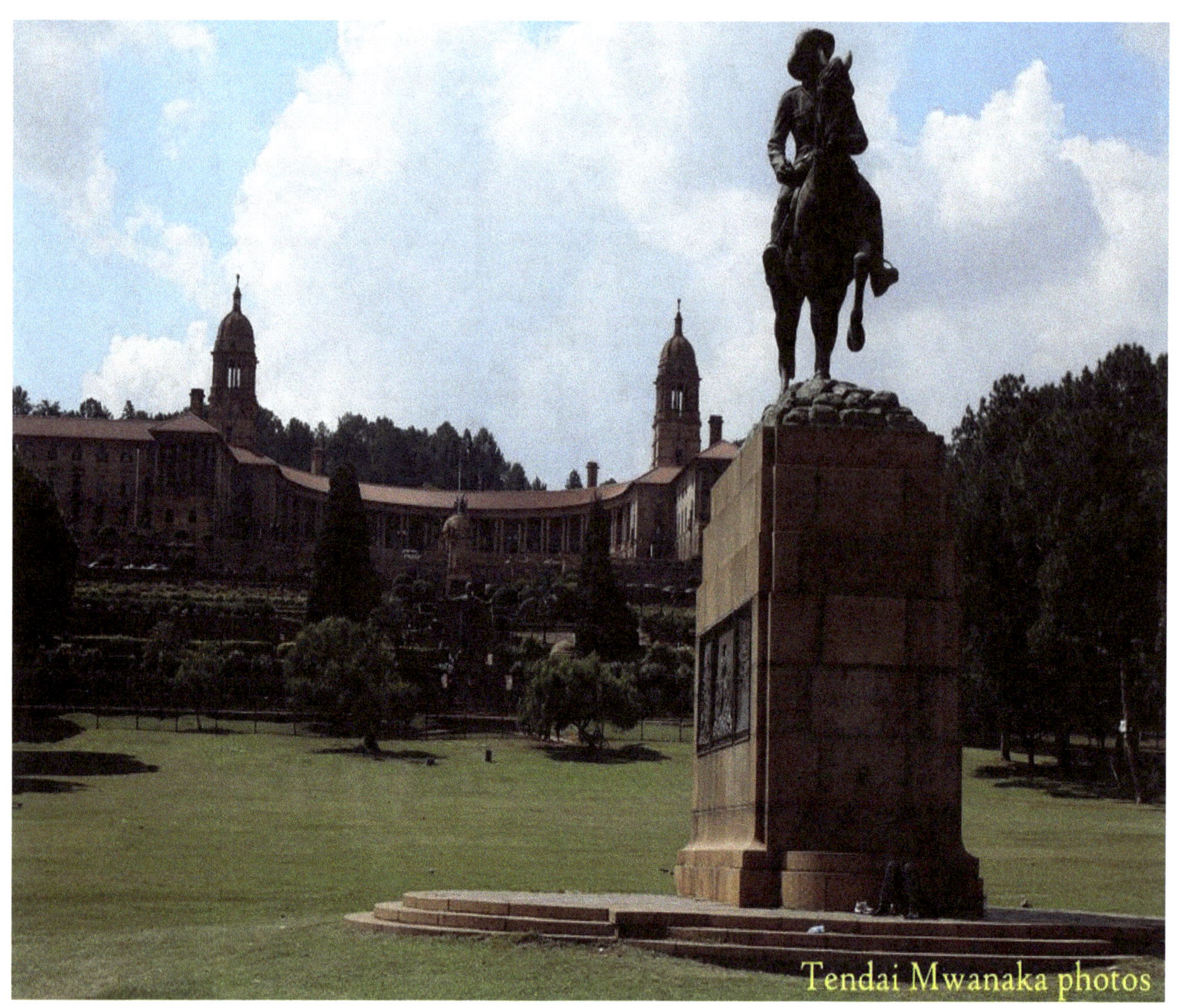

Union Buildings
2022

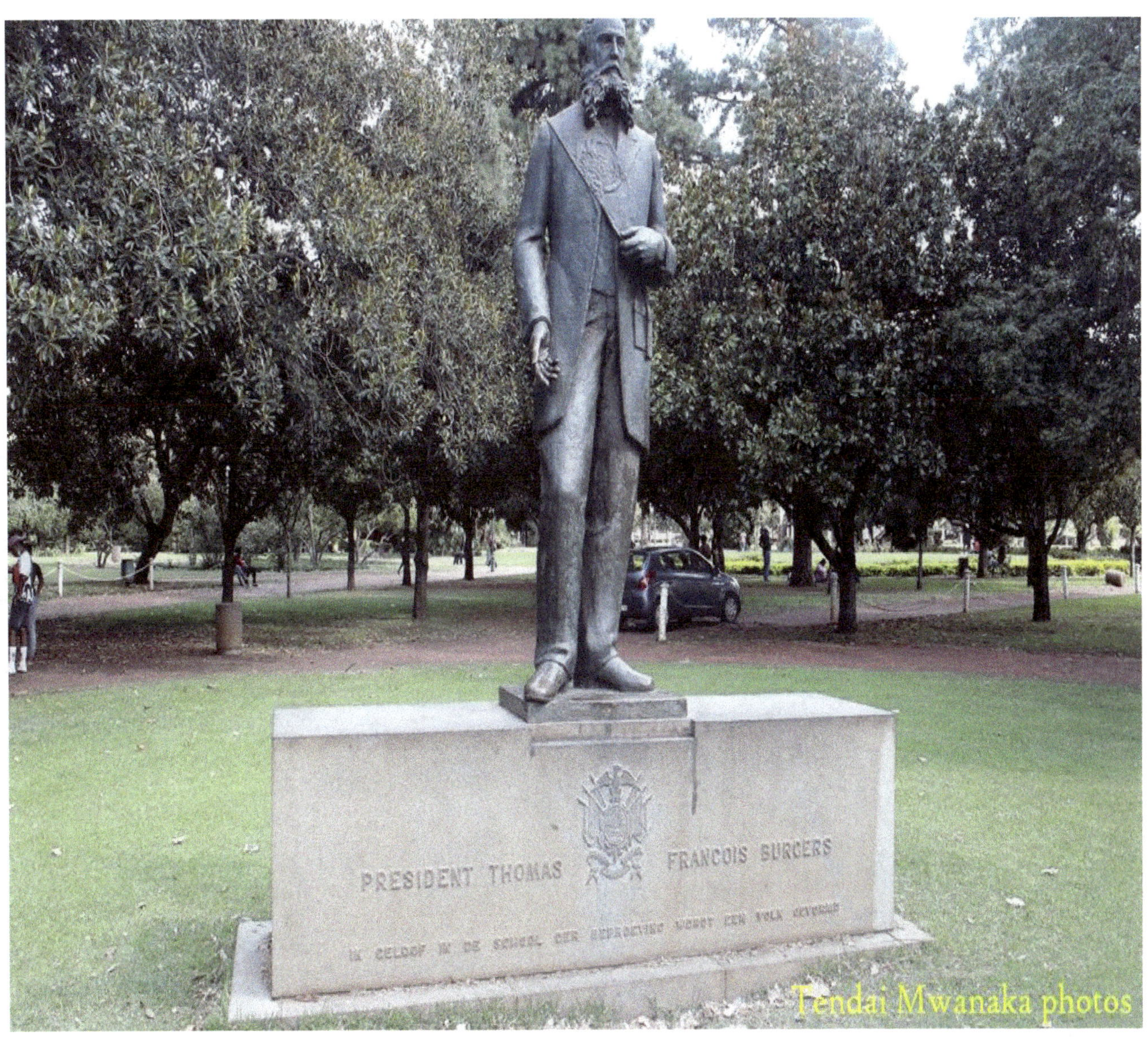

Burgers statue
2022

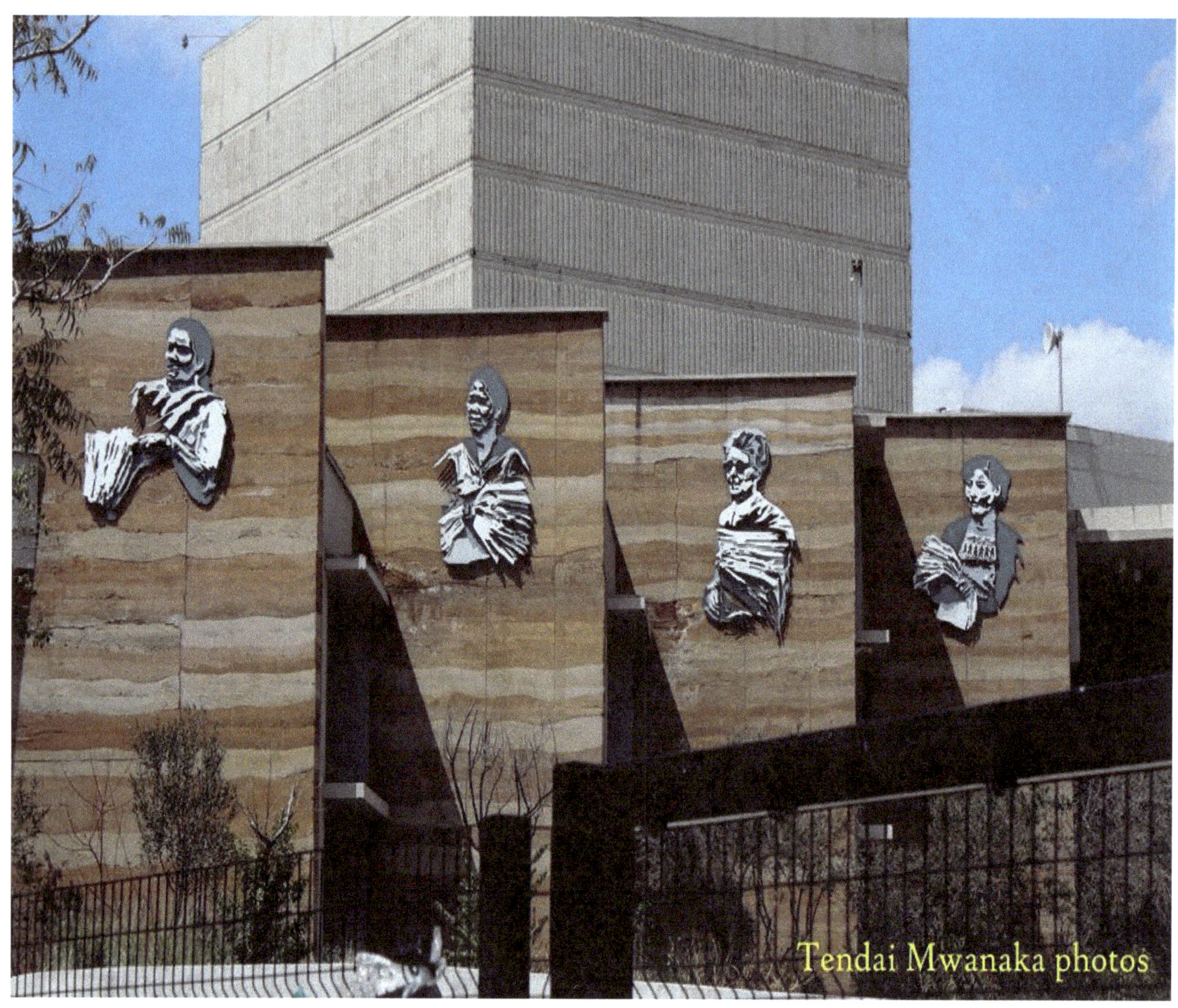

Accompanying Helen Suzman
2022

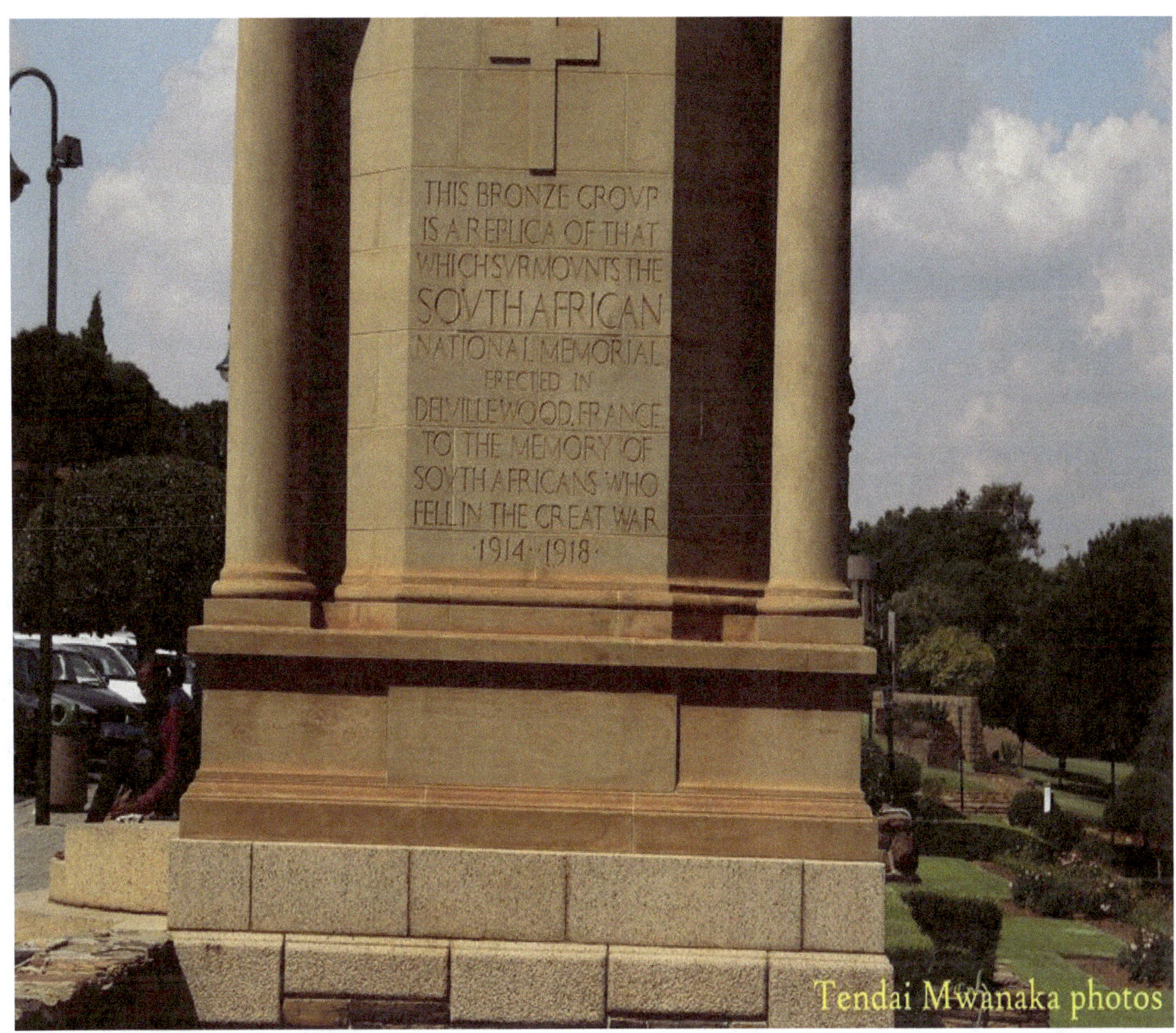

Lest we forget 2
2022

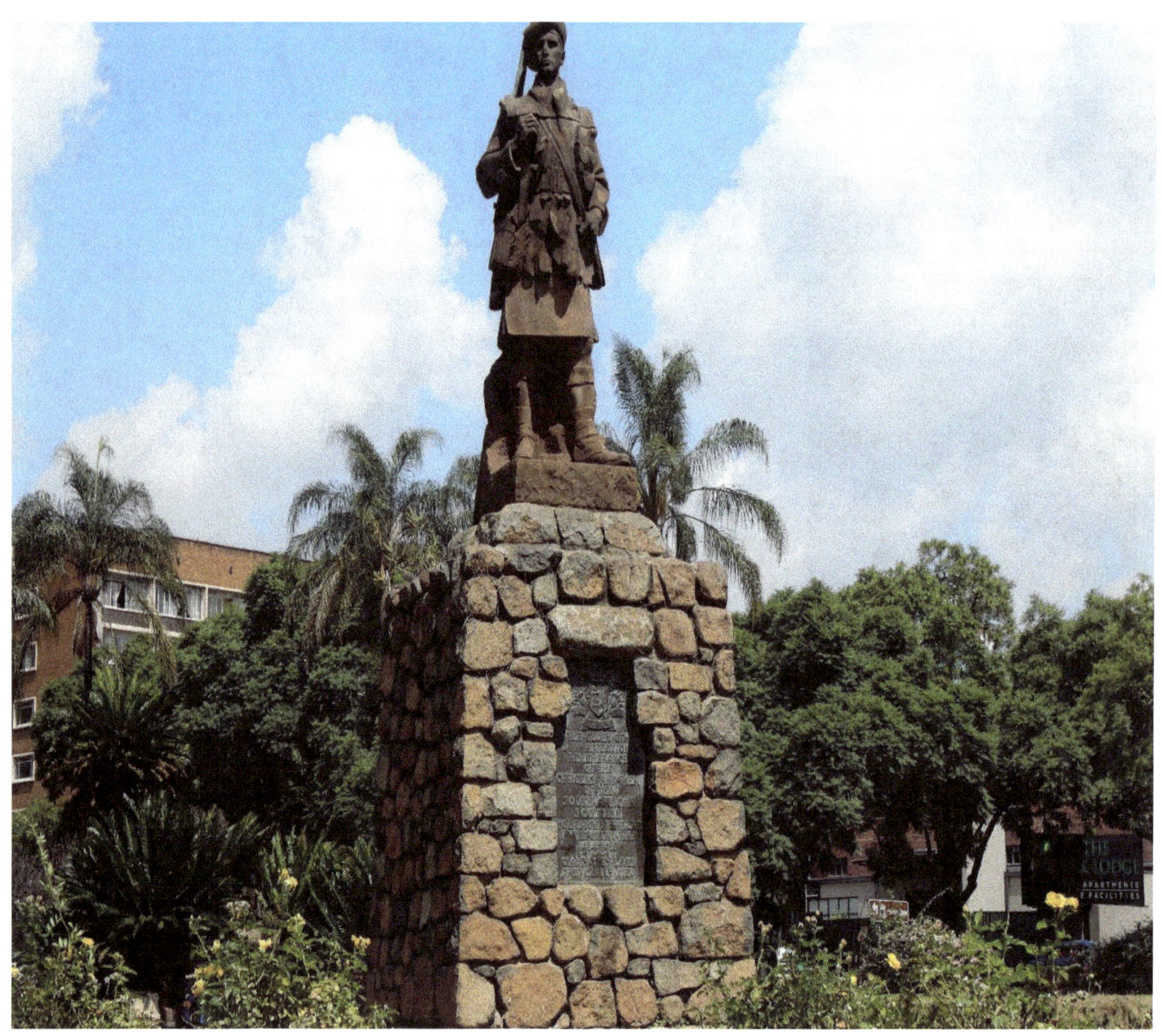

Accompanying Burgers
2022

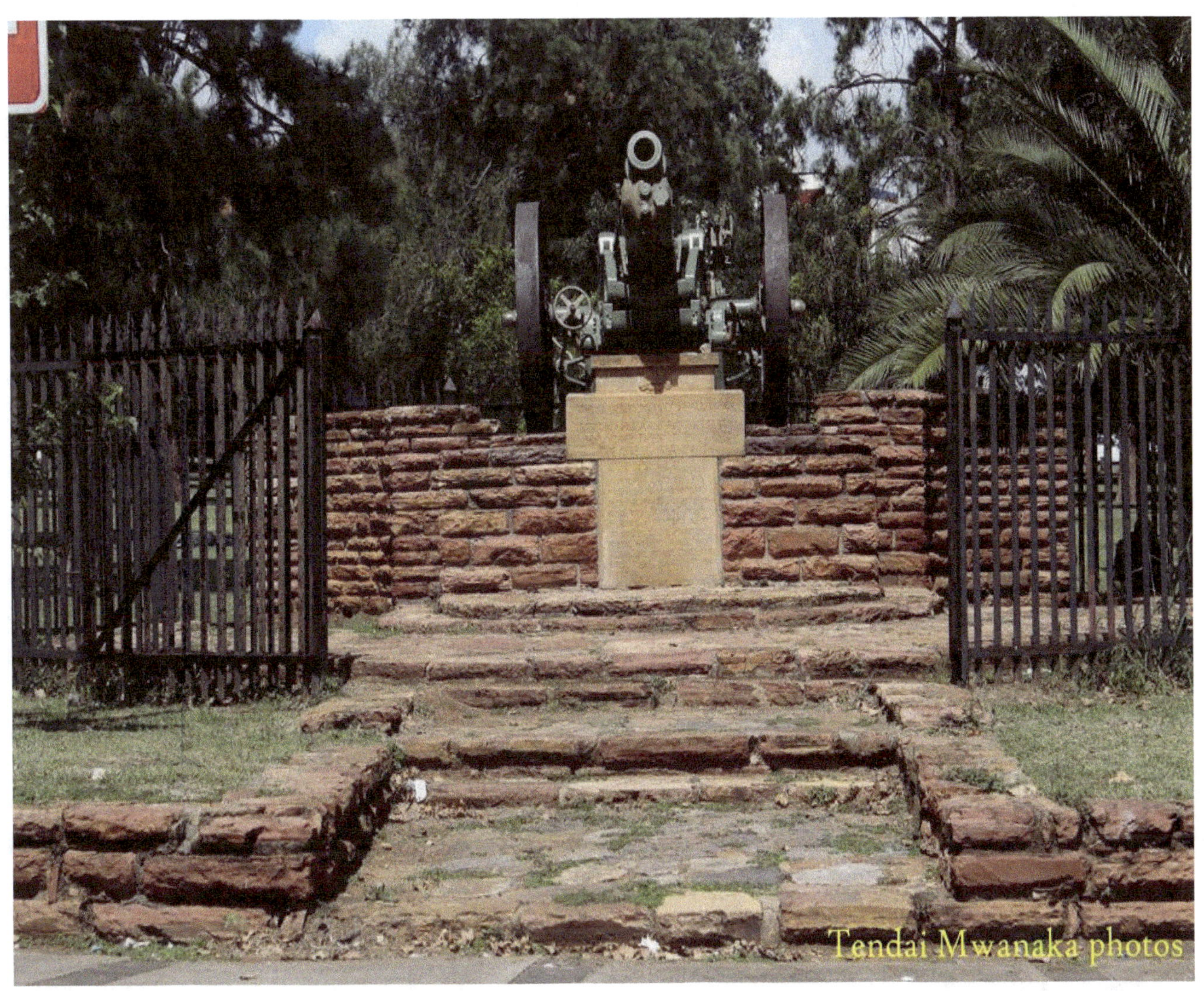

Artillery
2022

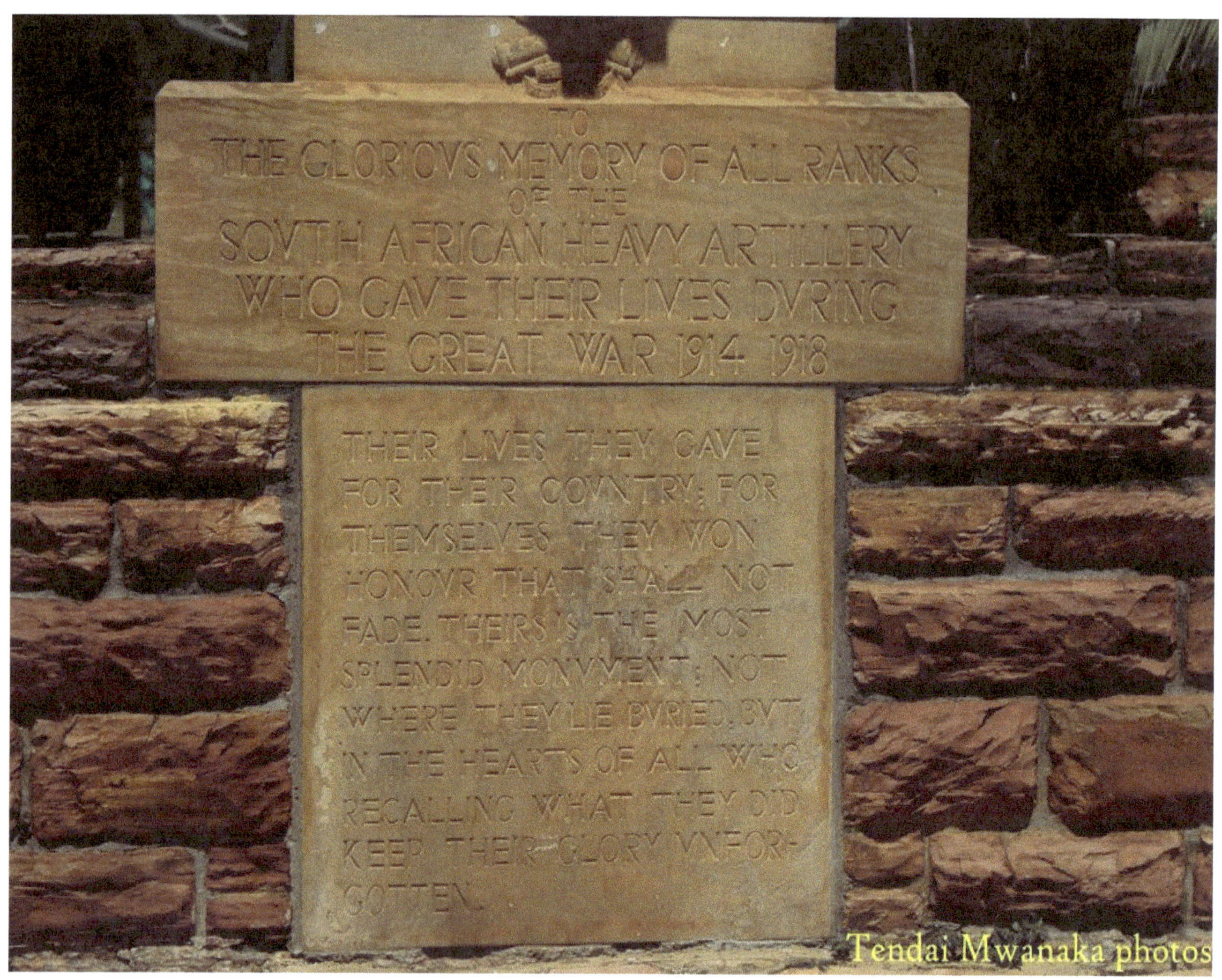

Lest we forget 1
2022

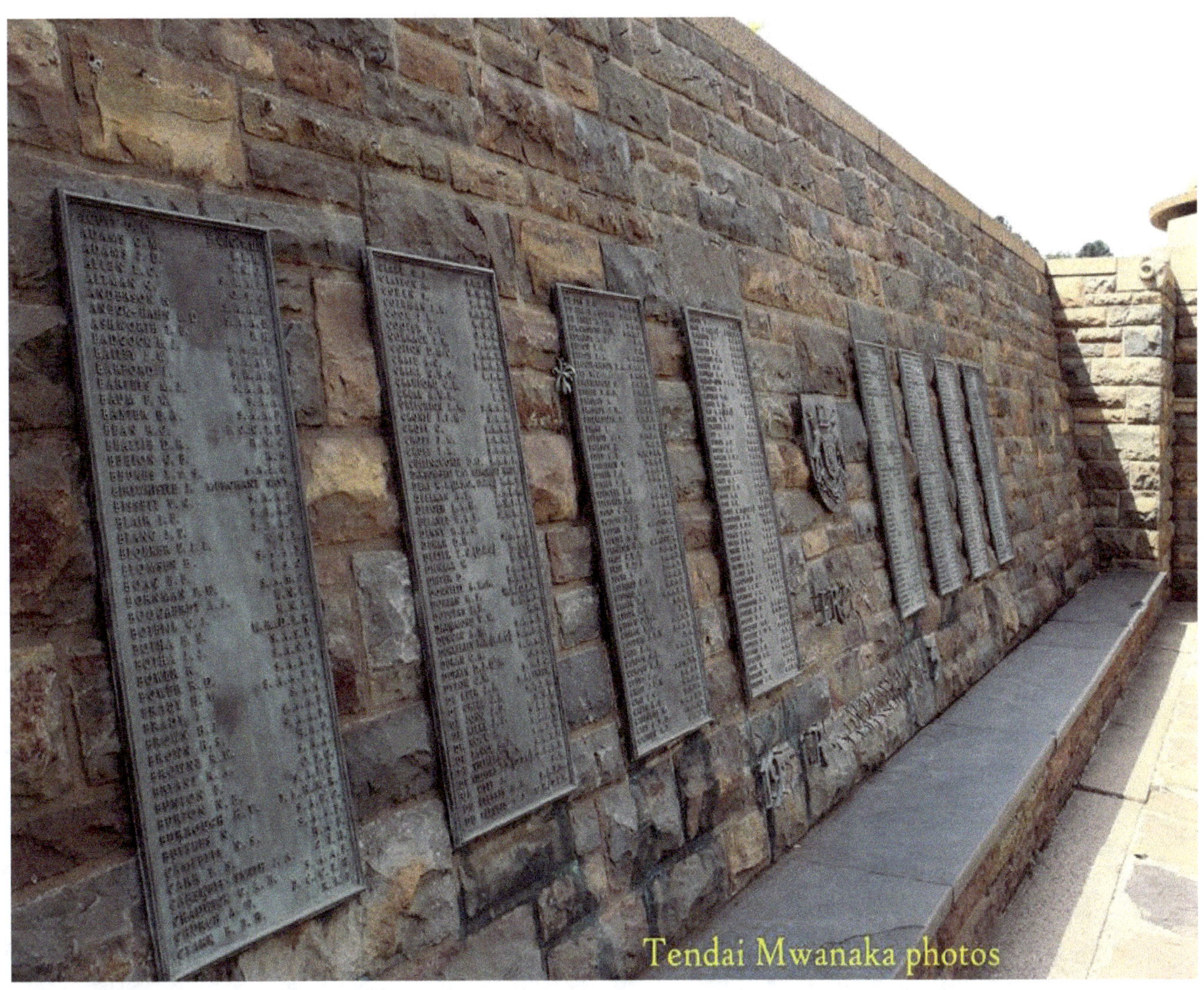

Honour Rolls
2022

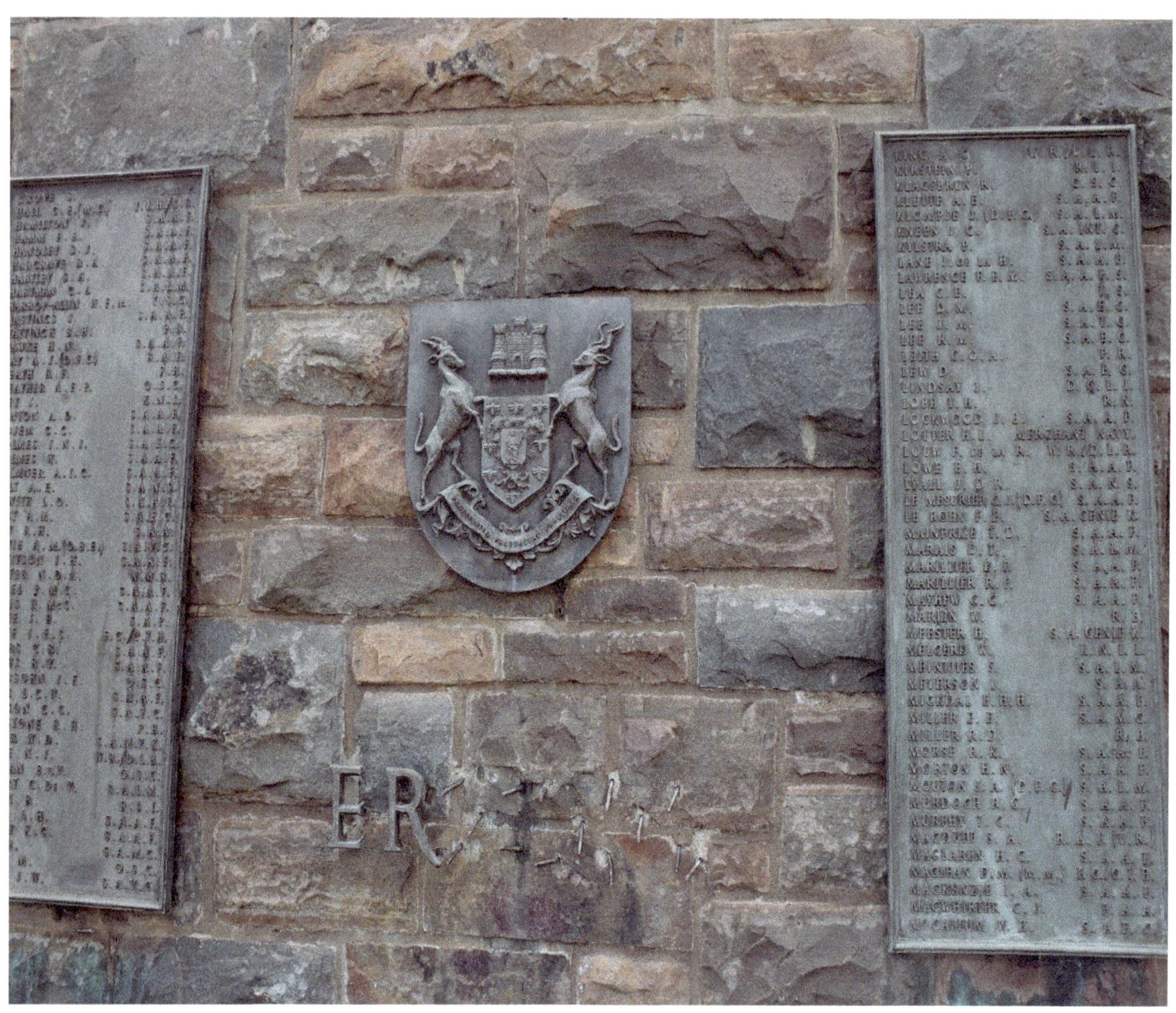

Honour roll upclose
2022

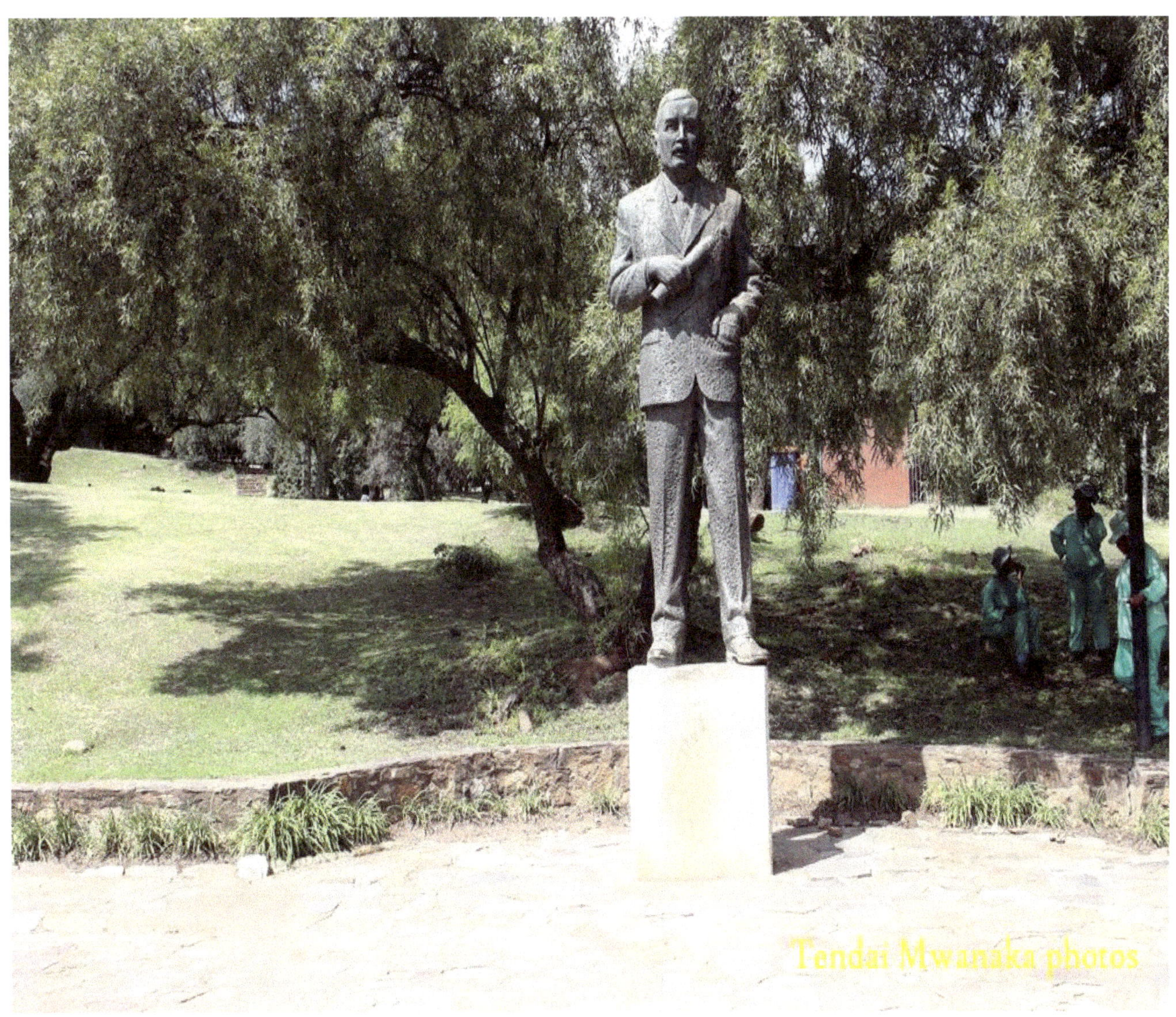

Move over Krueger, here comes Madiba
2022

HISTORY AND THE PRESENT

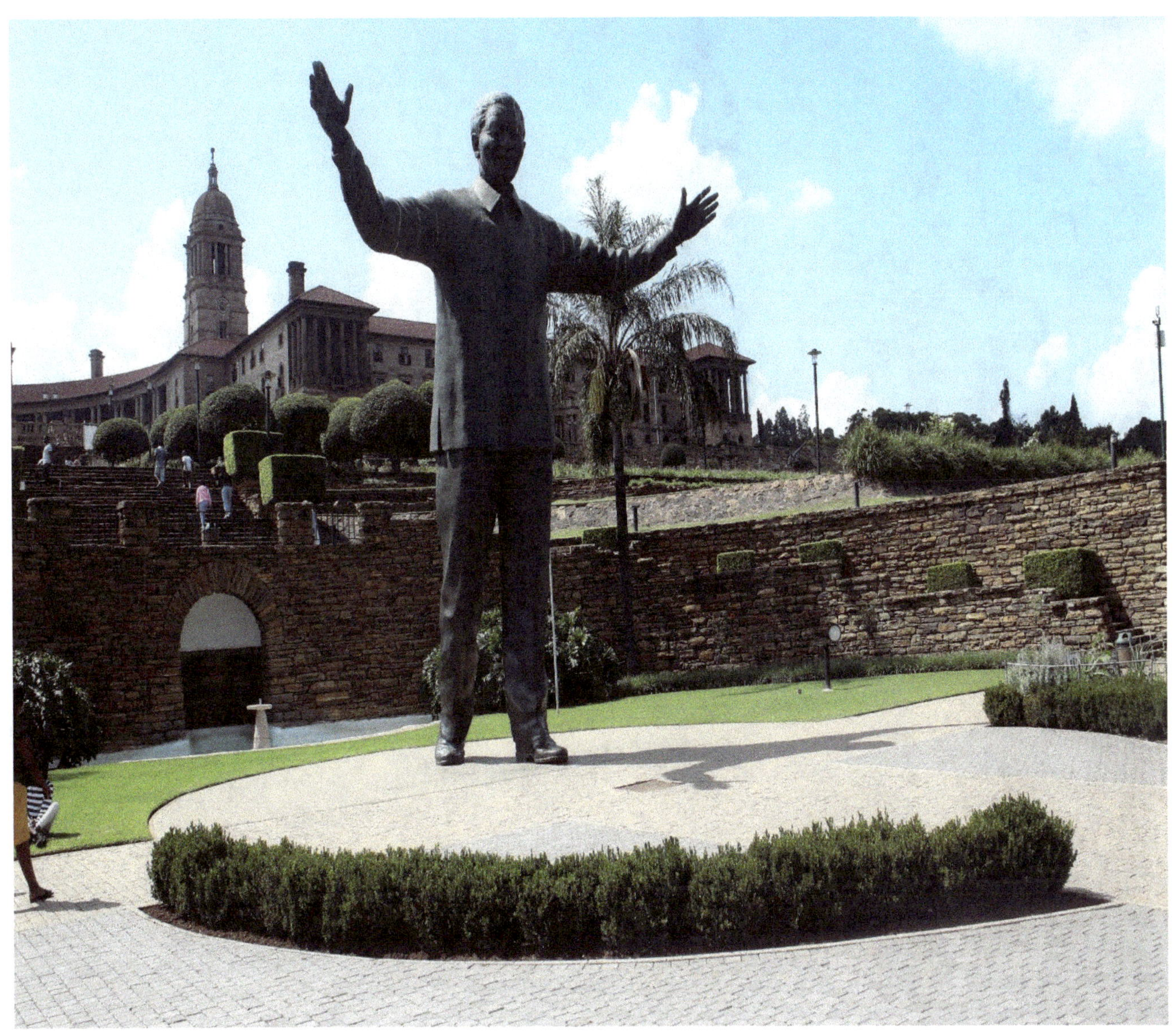

Open Arms
2022

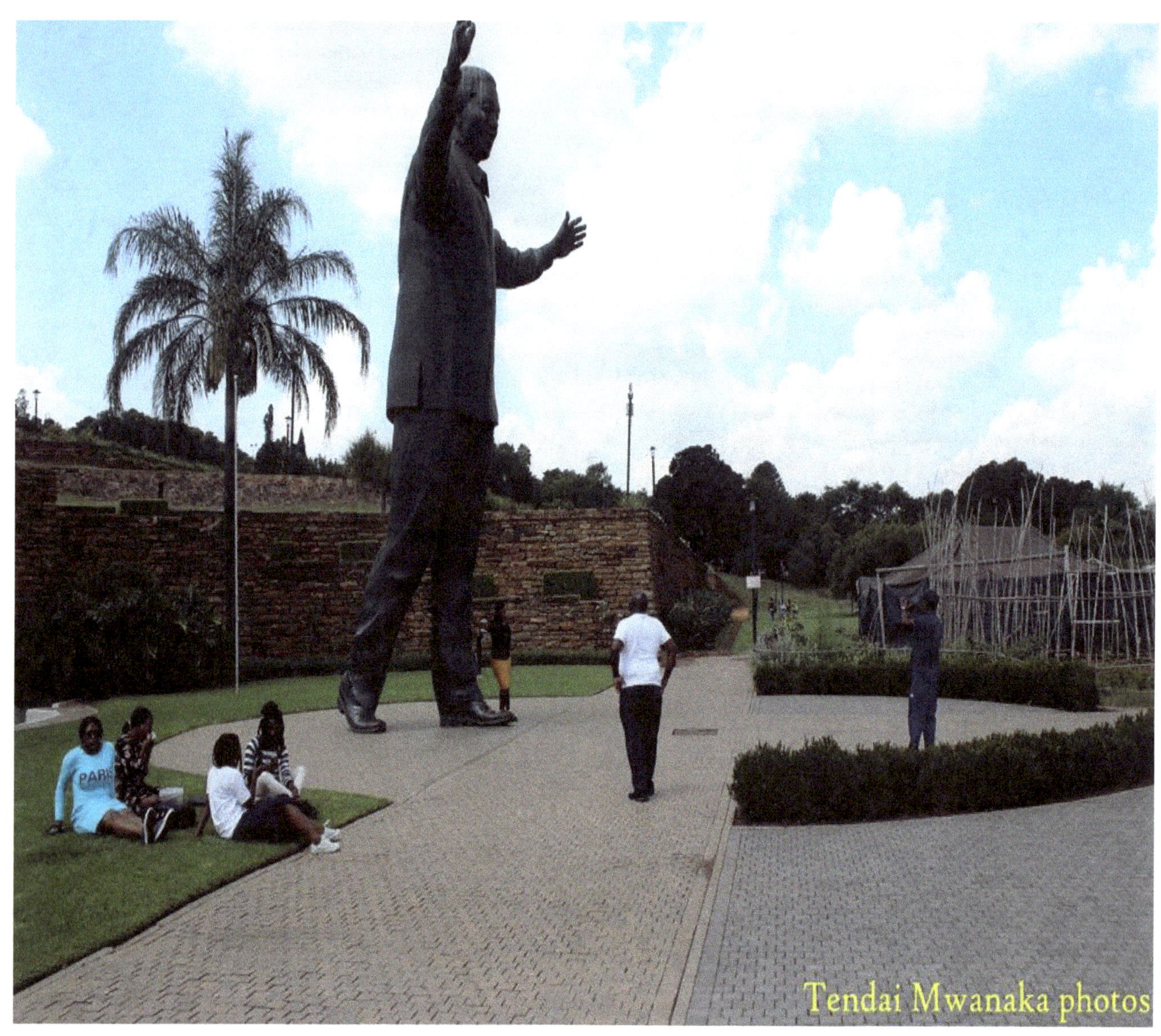

Madiba
2022

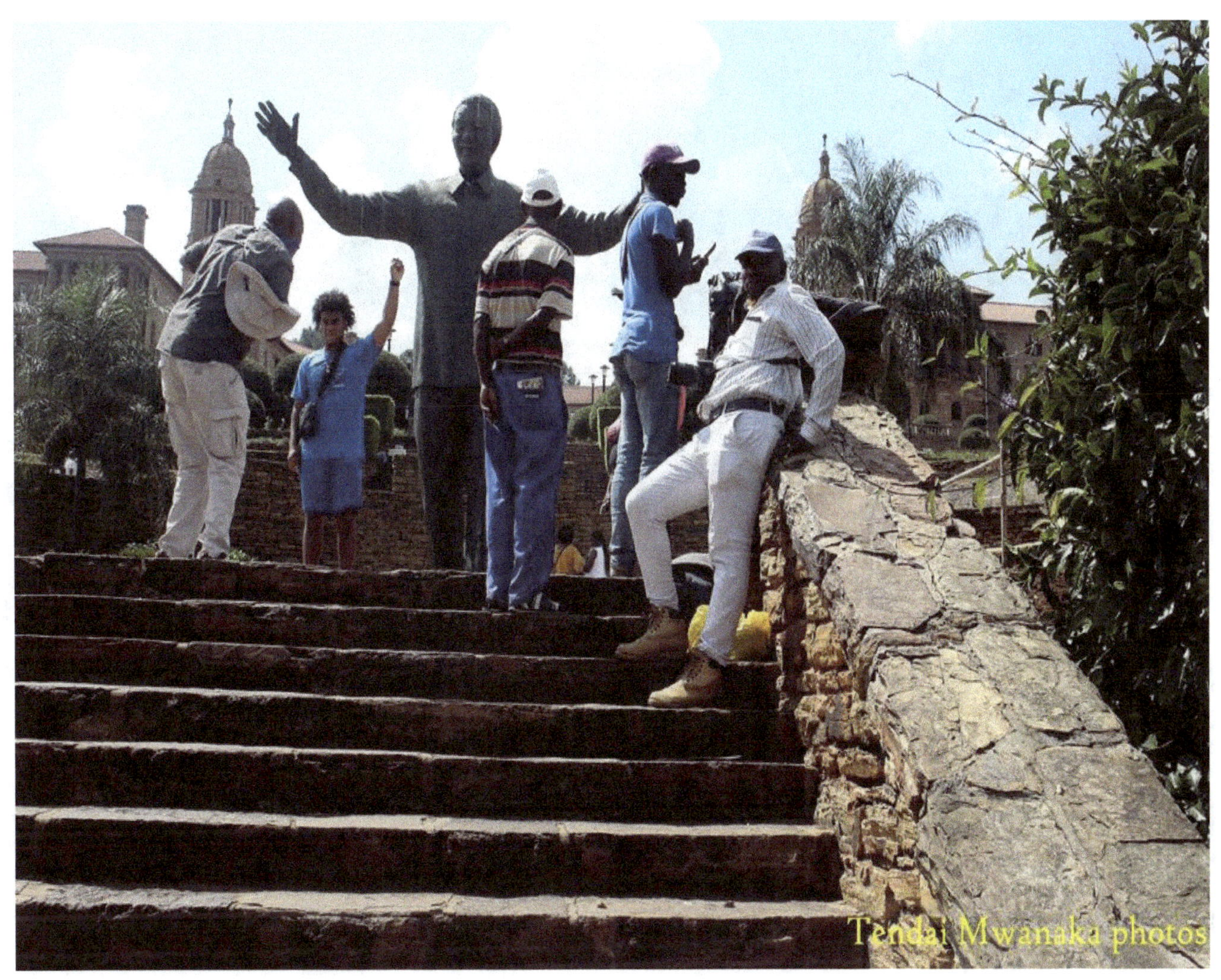

Amandla
2022

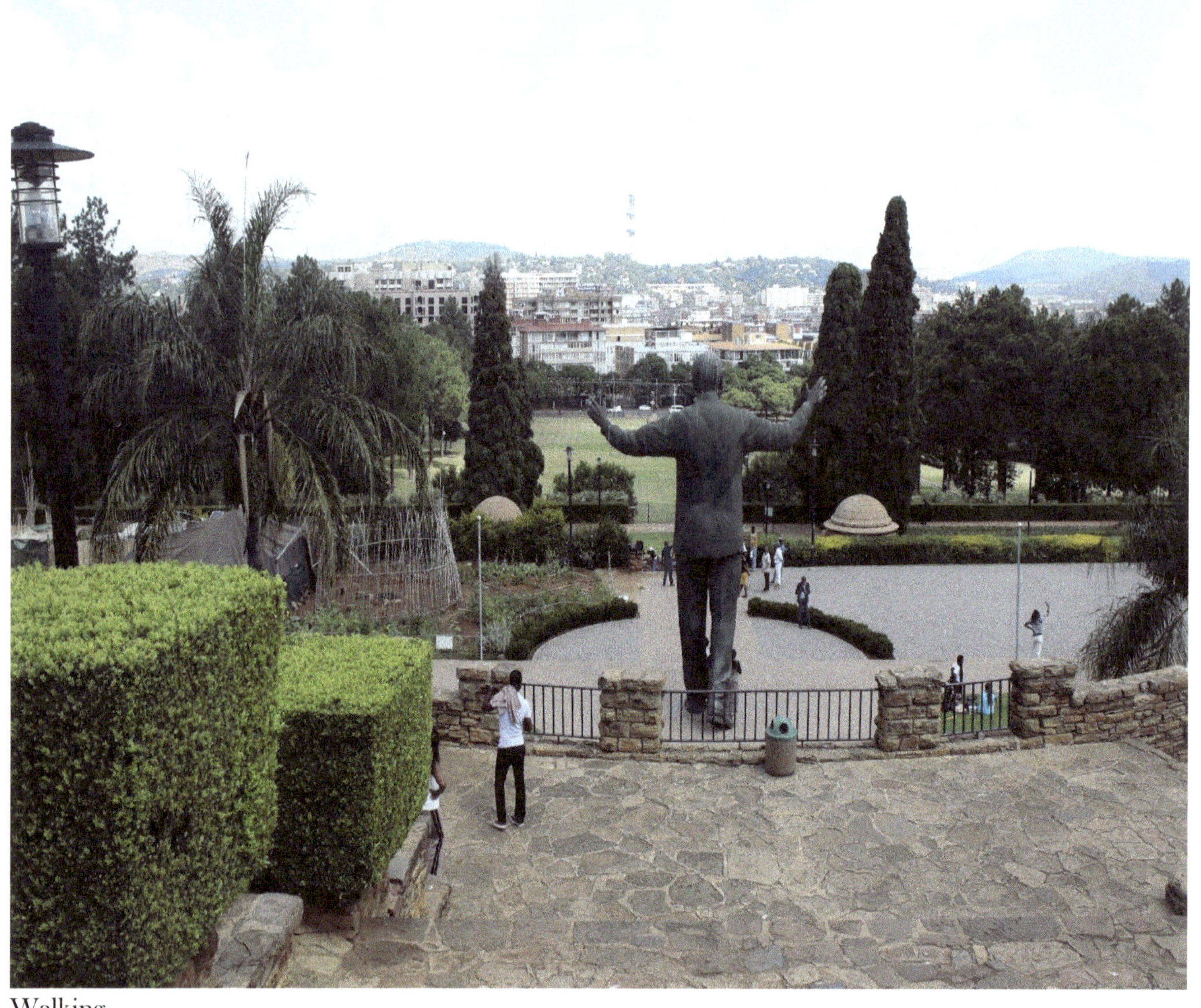

Walking
2022

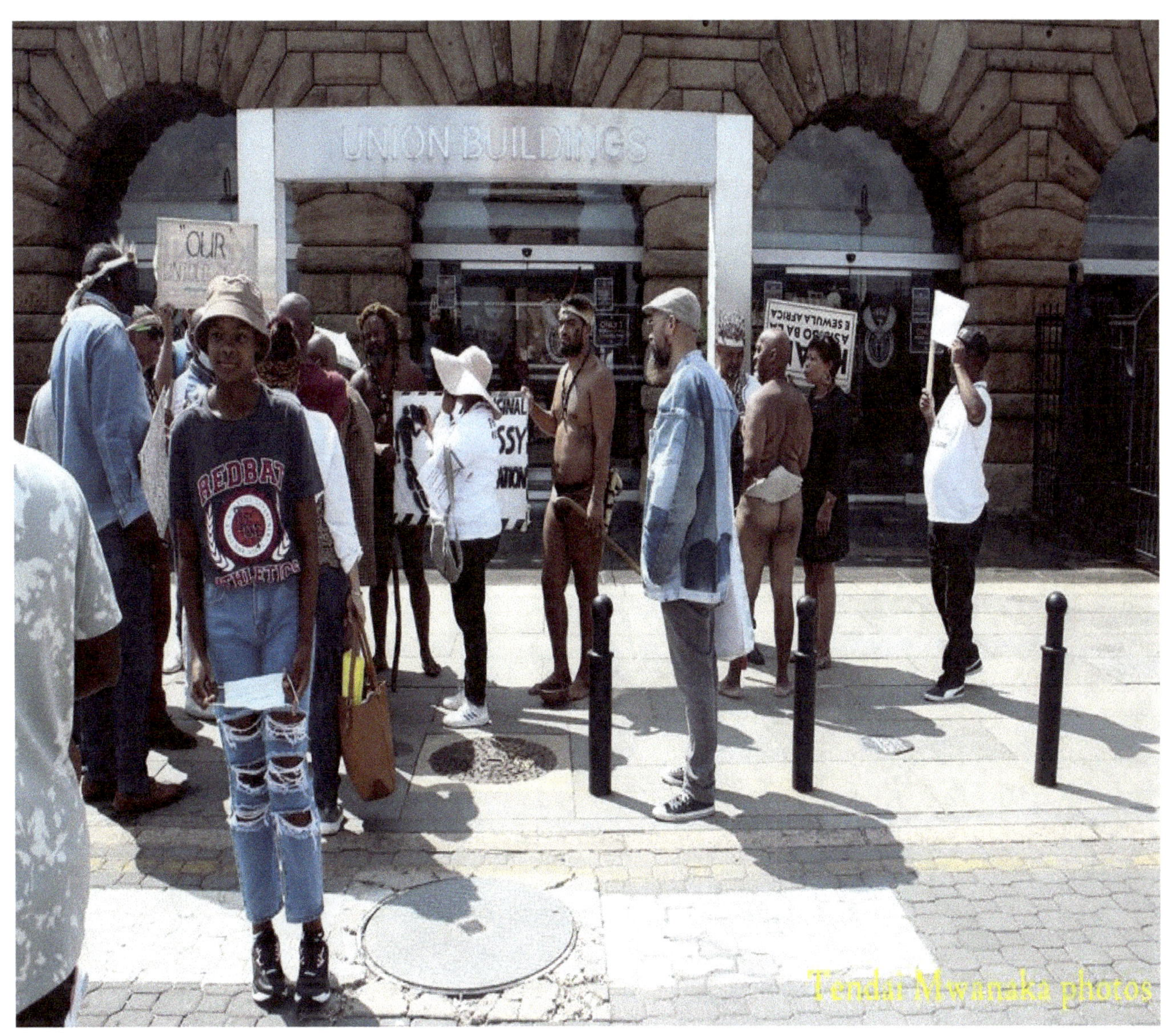

Standing up to power
2022

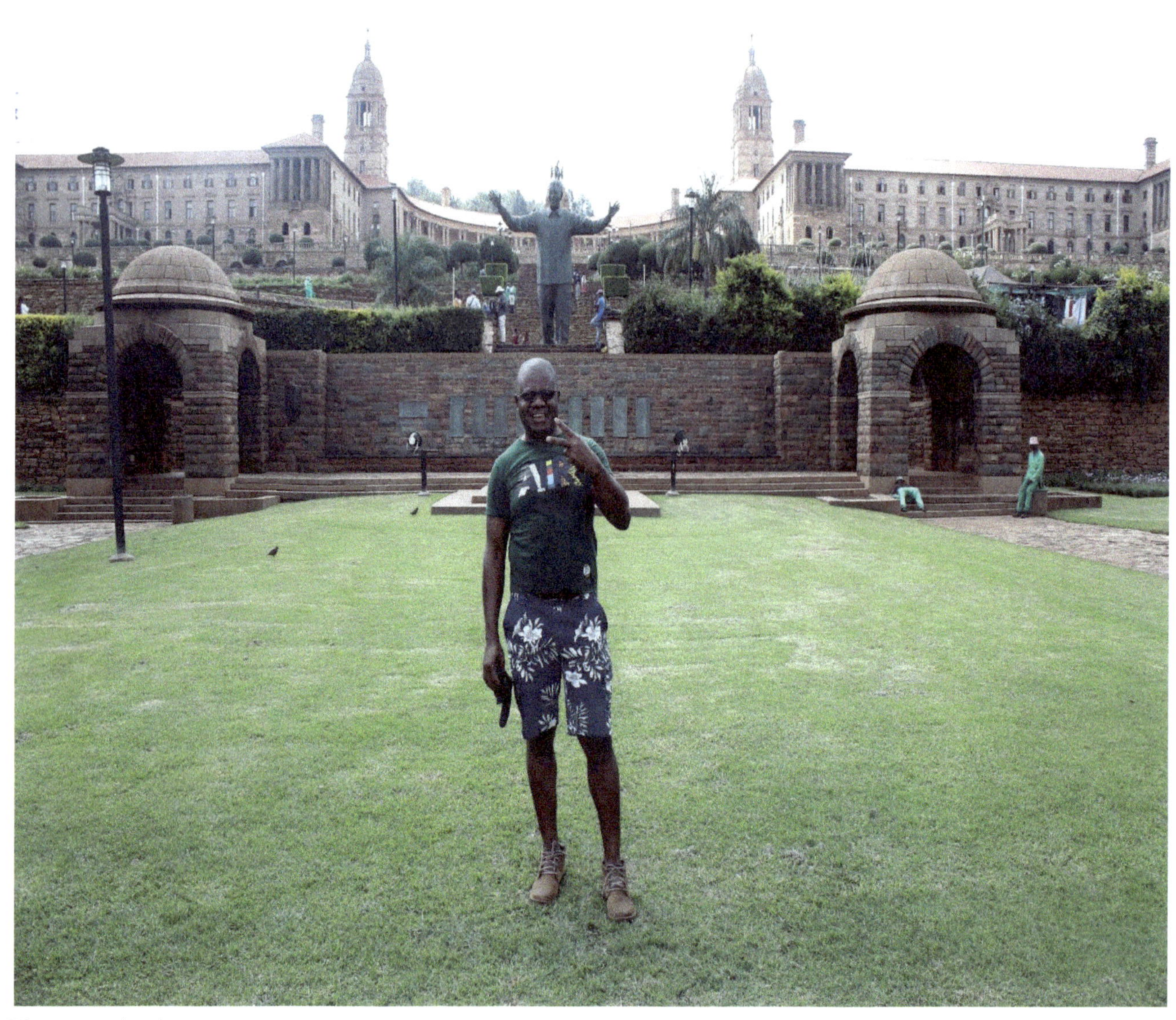

Photographer's pose
2022

ARCHITECTURAL MUSIC

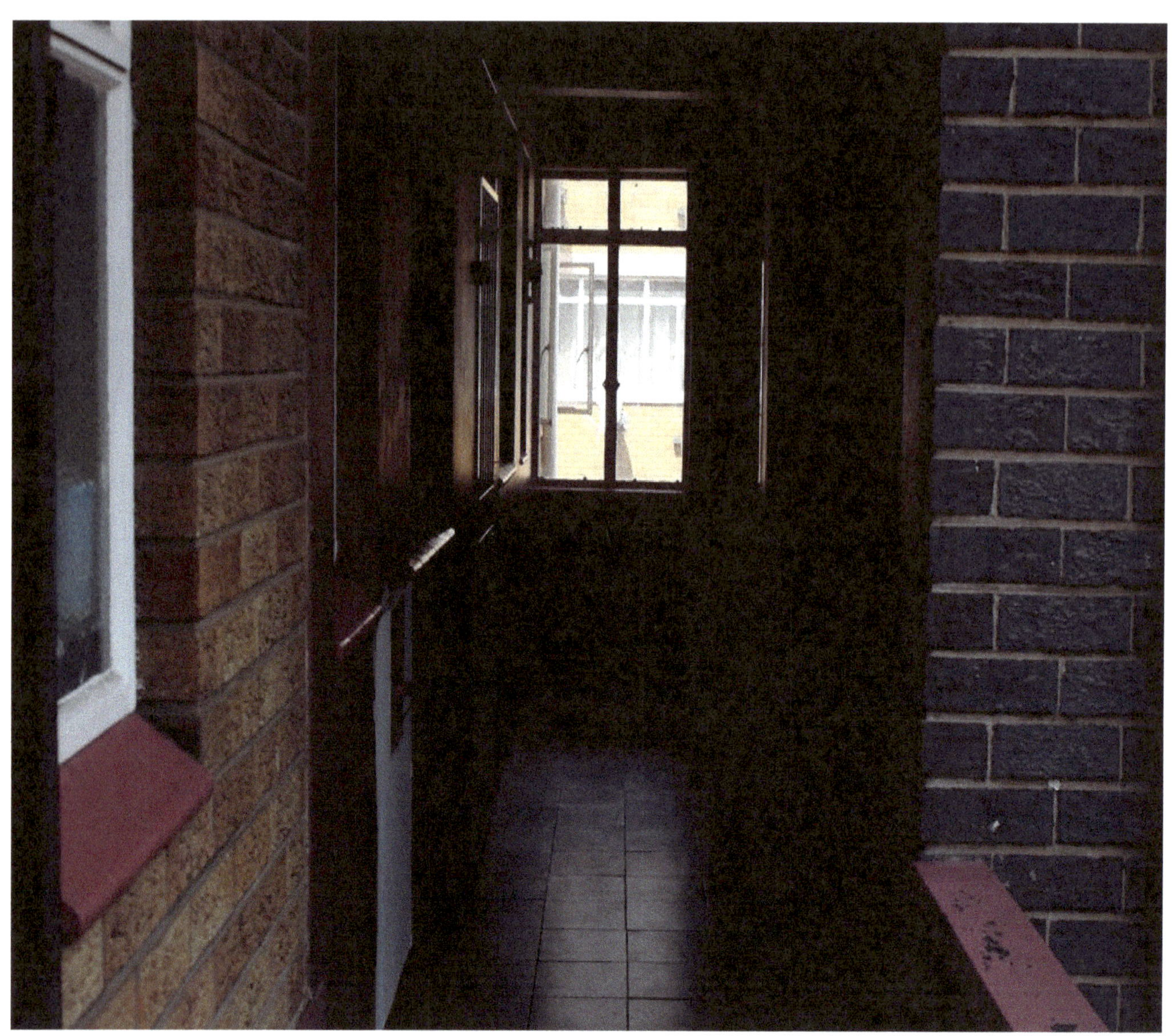

Entering
2022

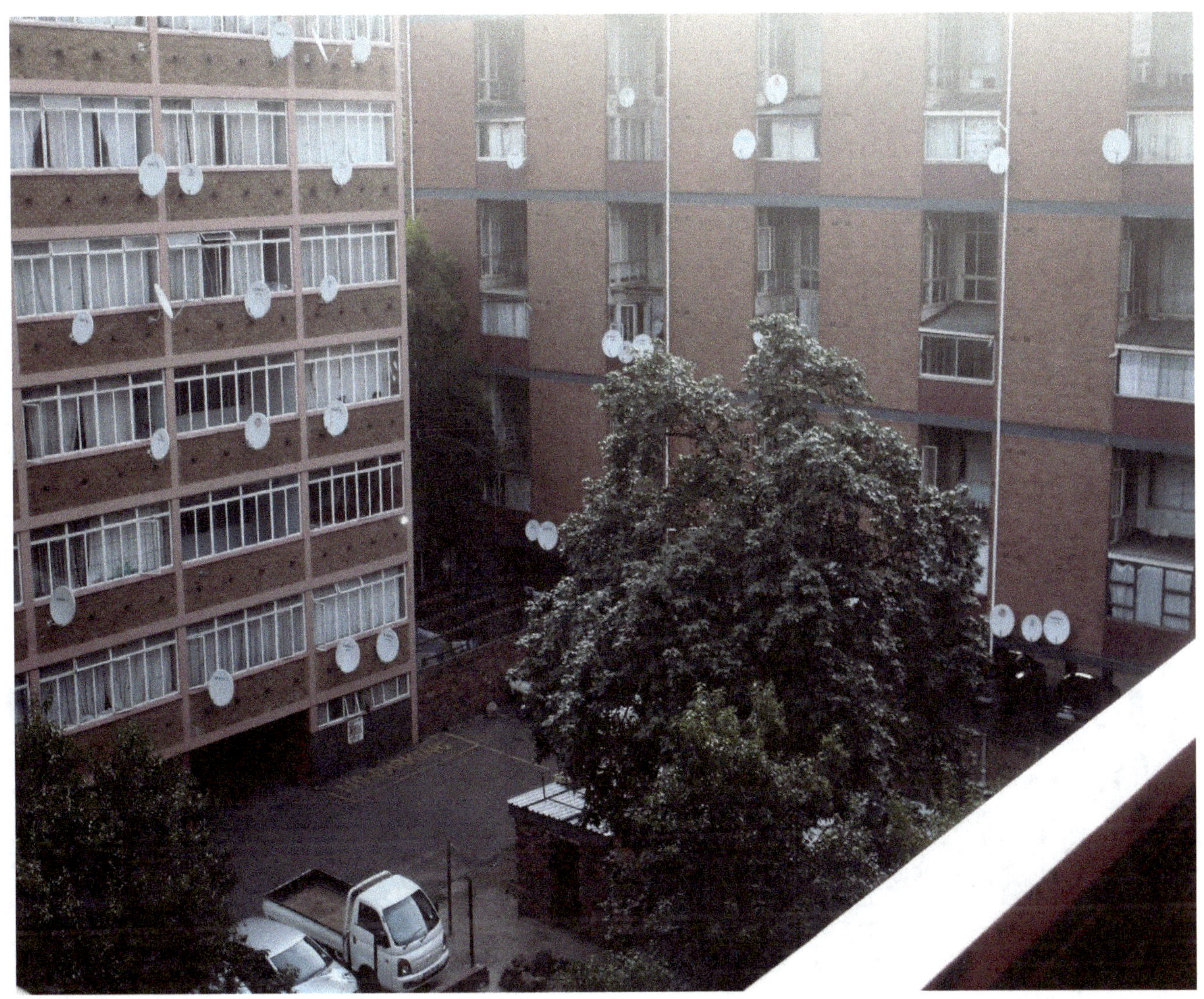

Enclosure
2022

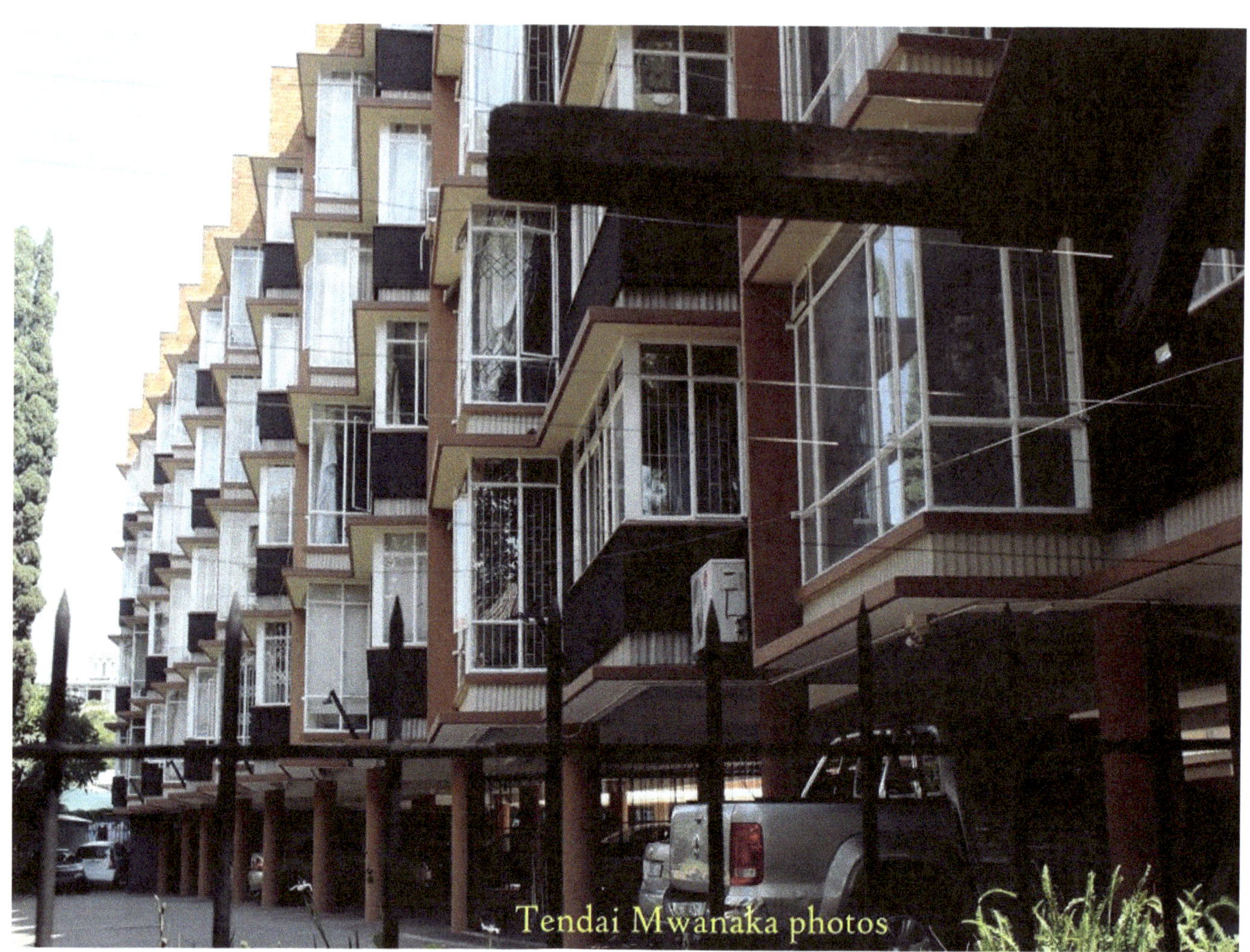

The act of carrying
2022

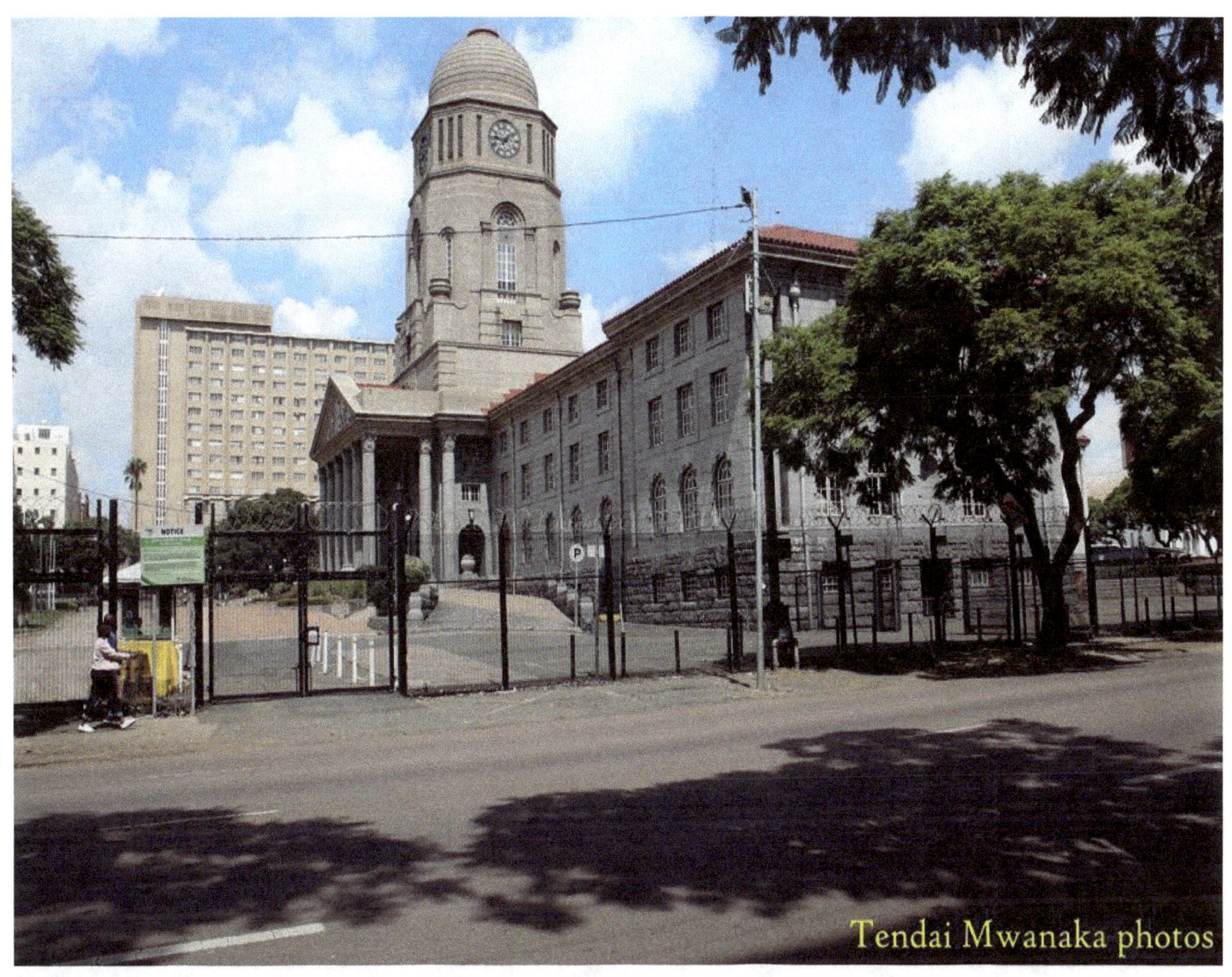

City hall
2022

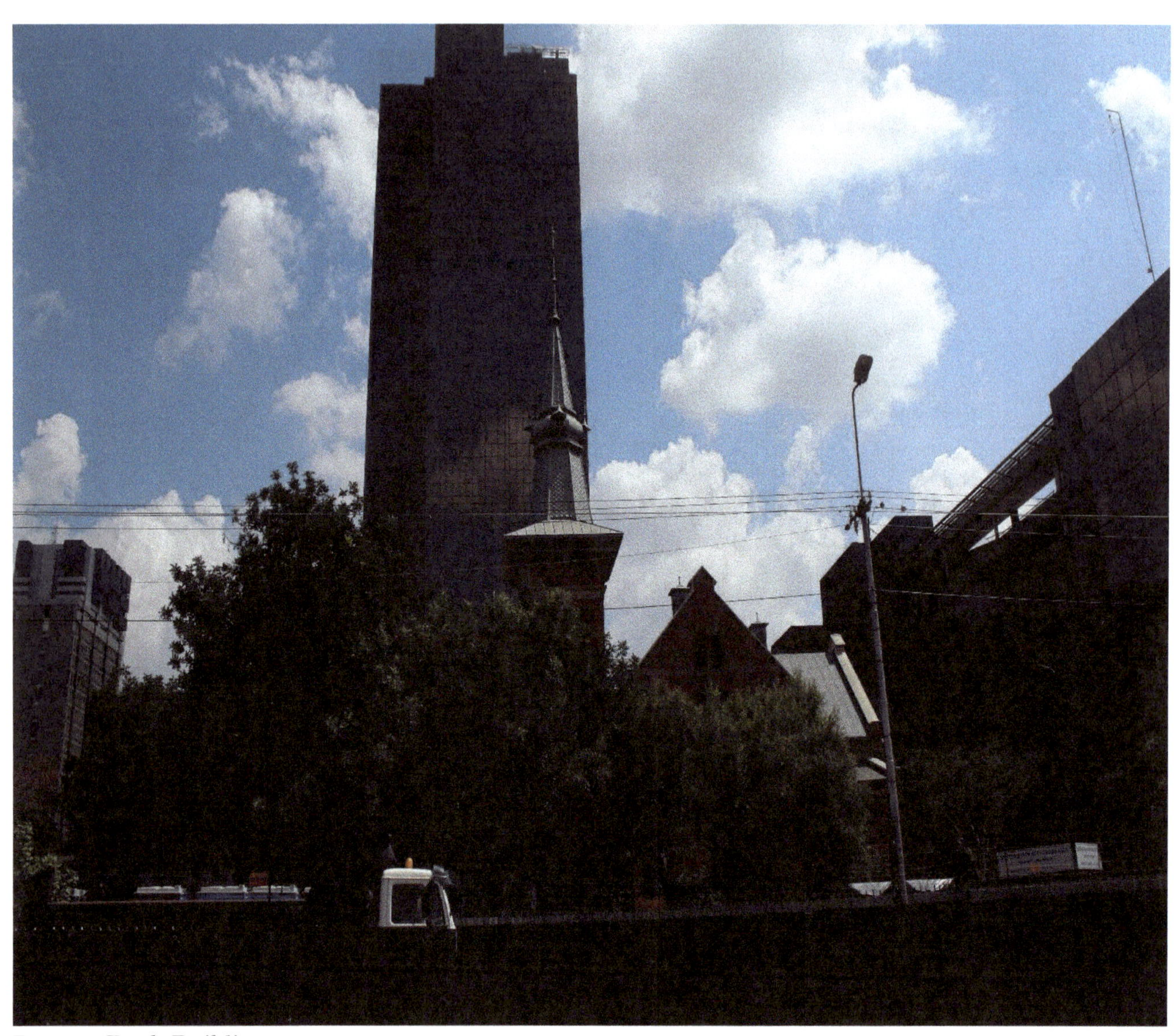

Reserve Bank Building
2022

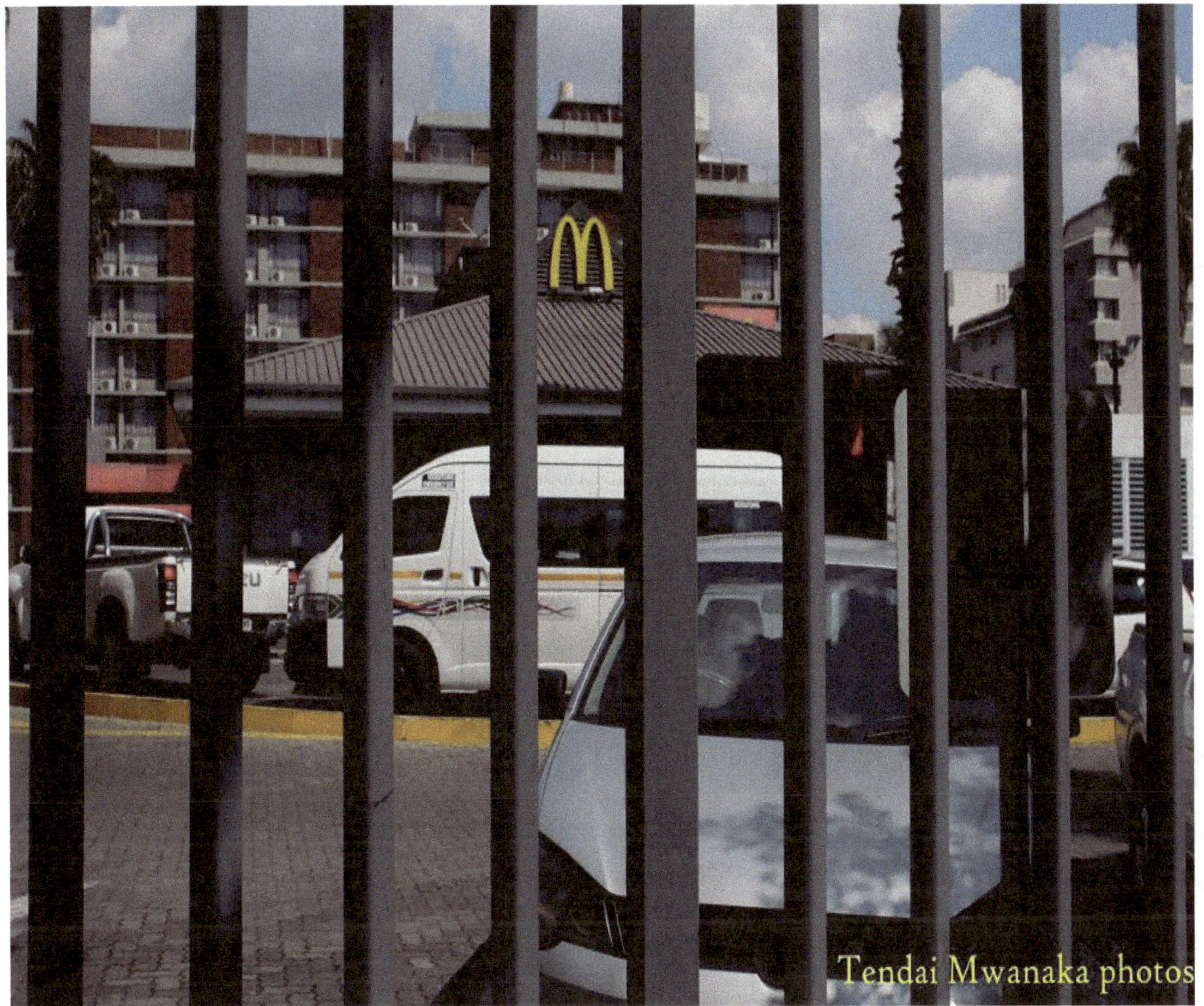

Big Mac
2022

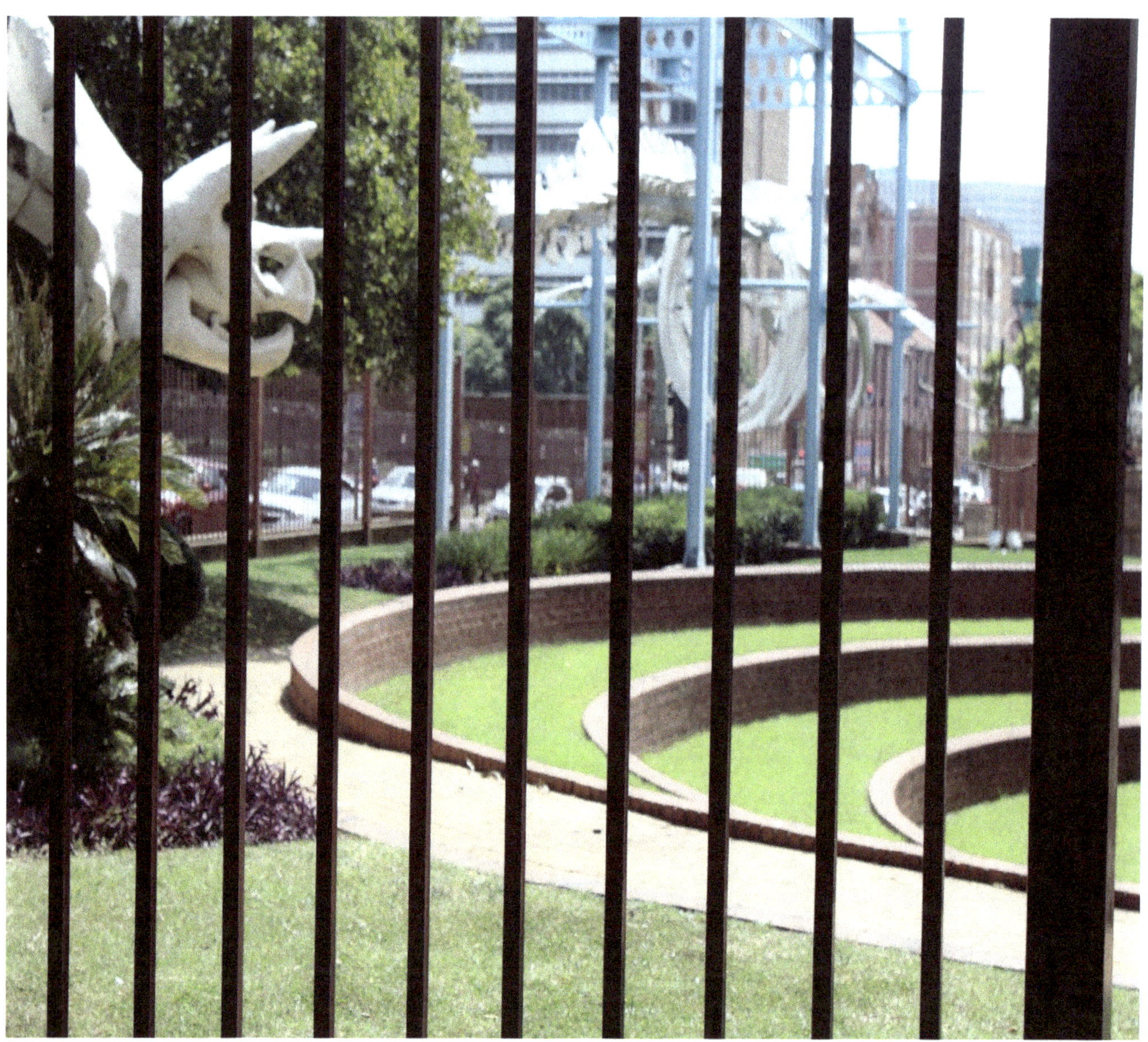

Lines
2022

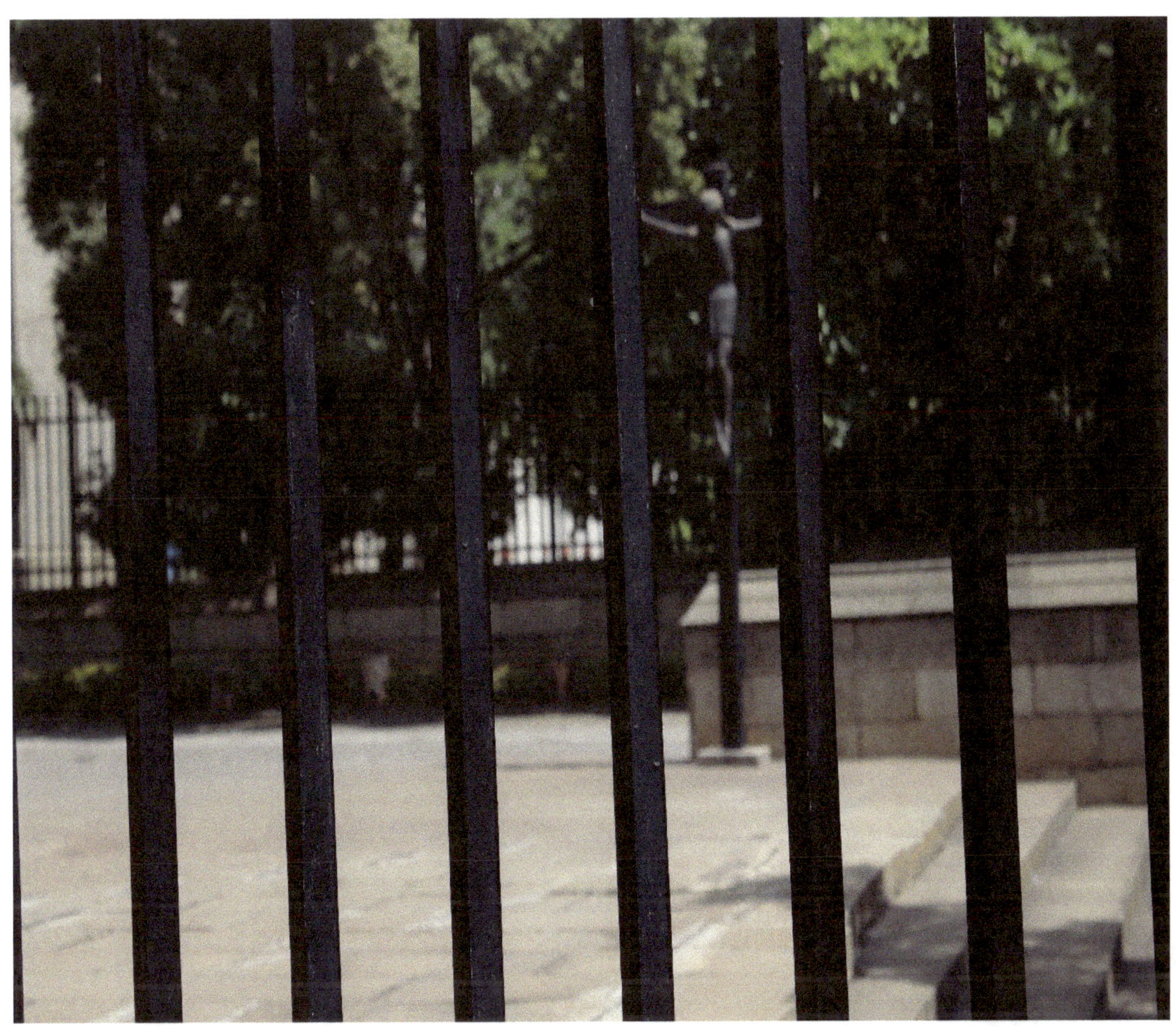

Imprisoned Jesus
2022

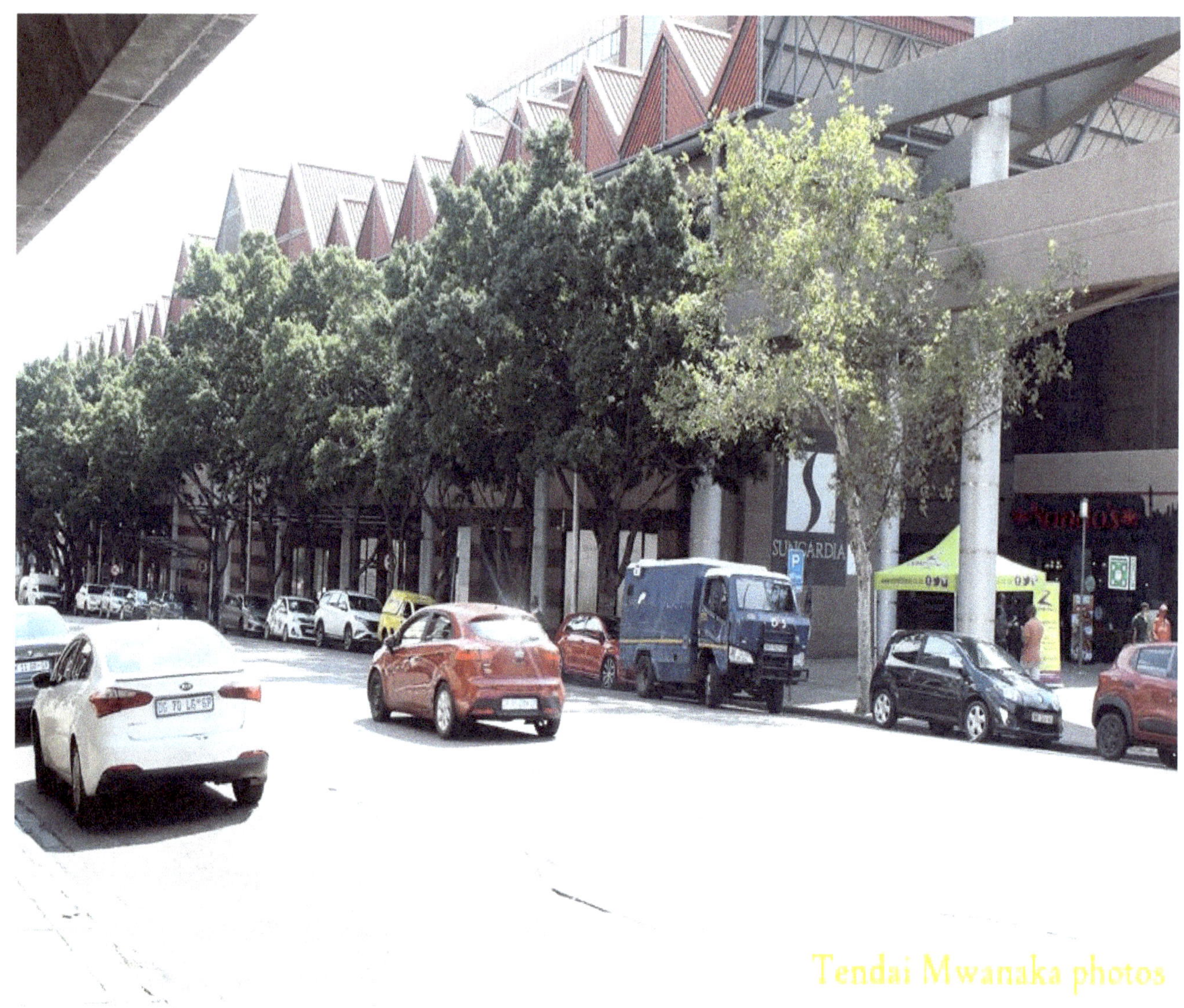

Triangular music
2022

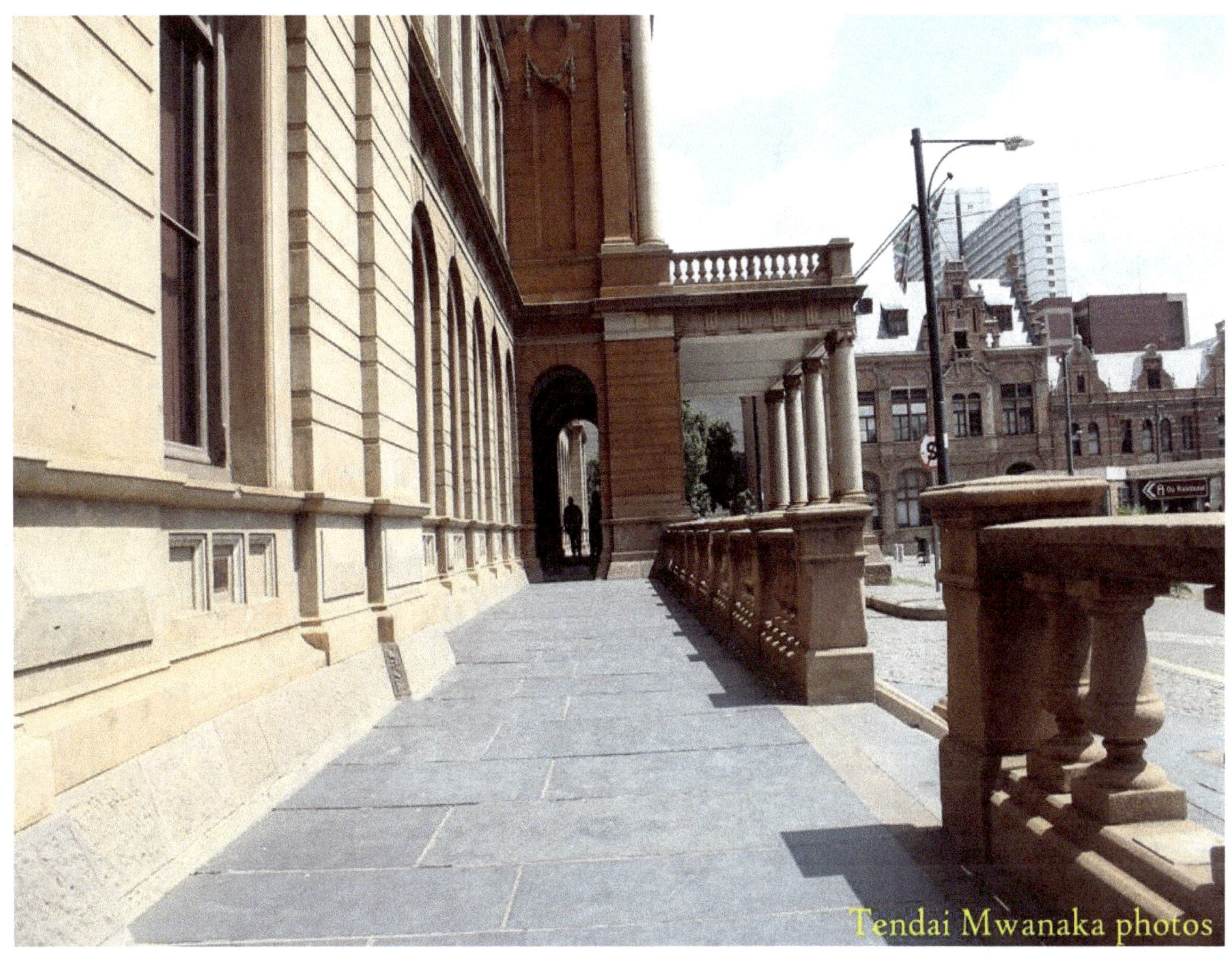

The way we are in
2022

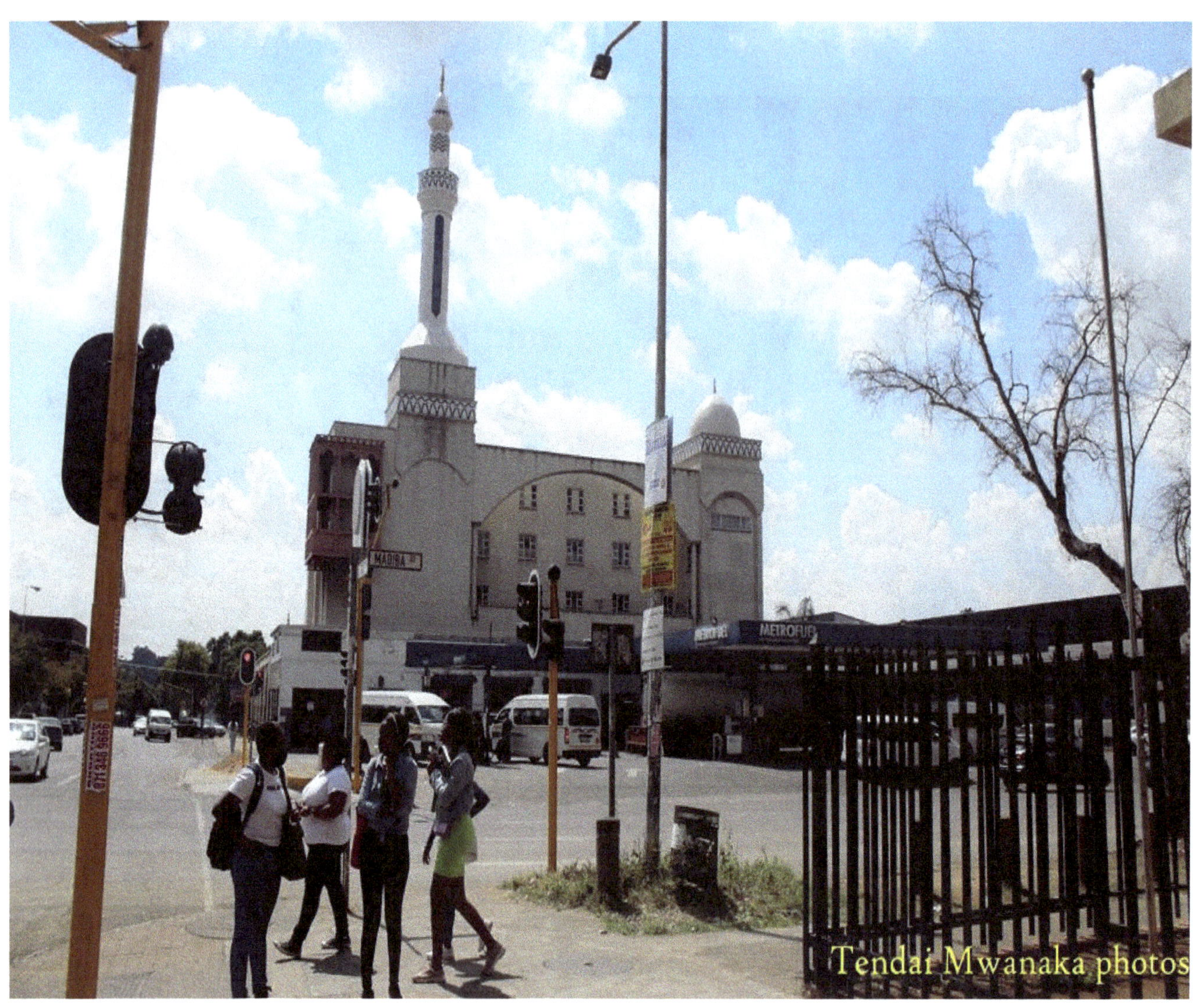

Temples of our hearts
2022

STREETS OF PRETORIA

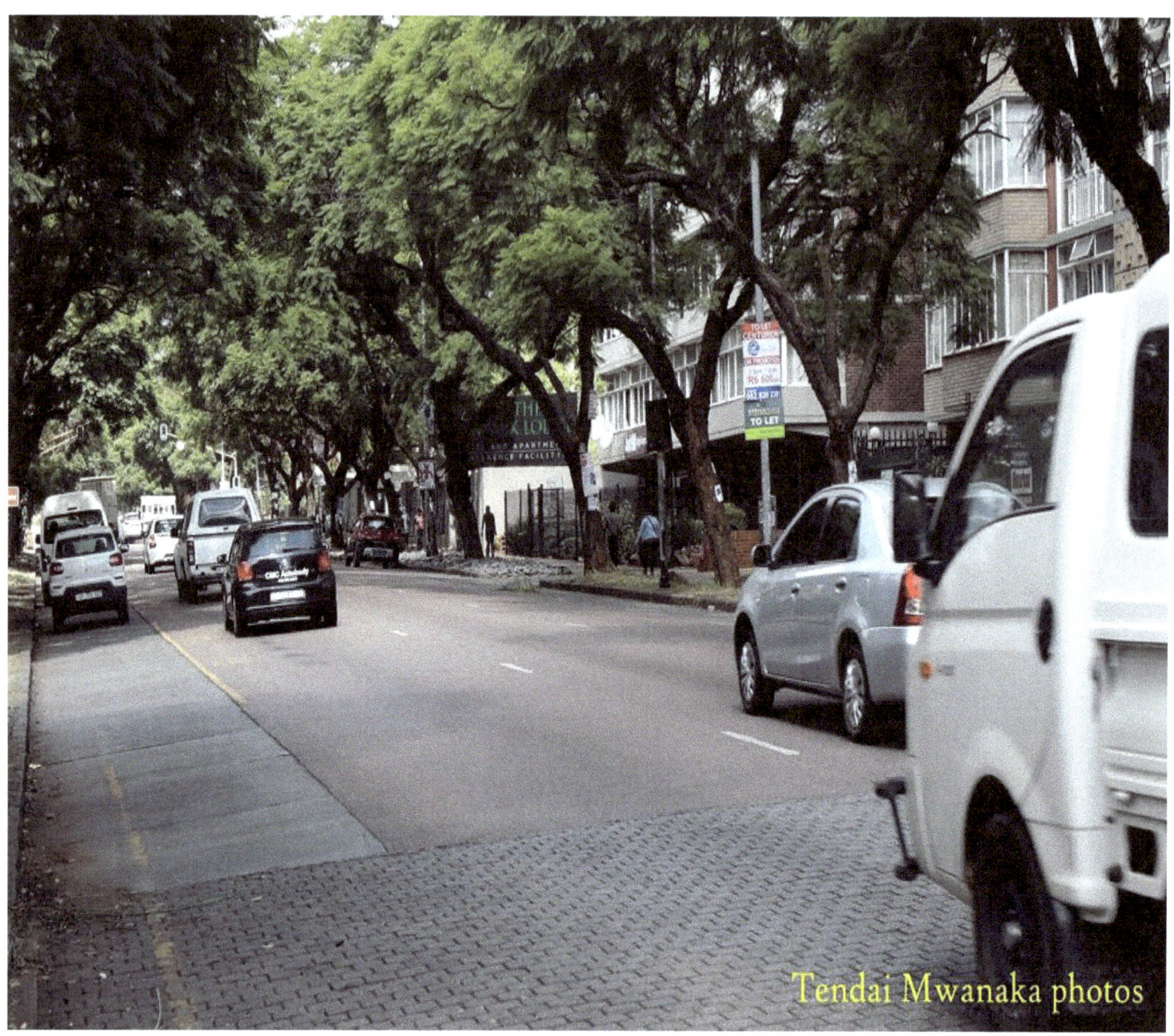

Bosman Avenue
2022

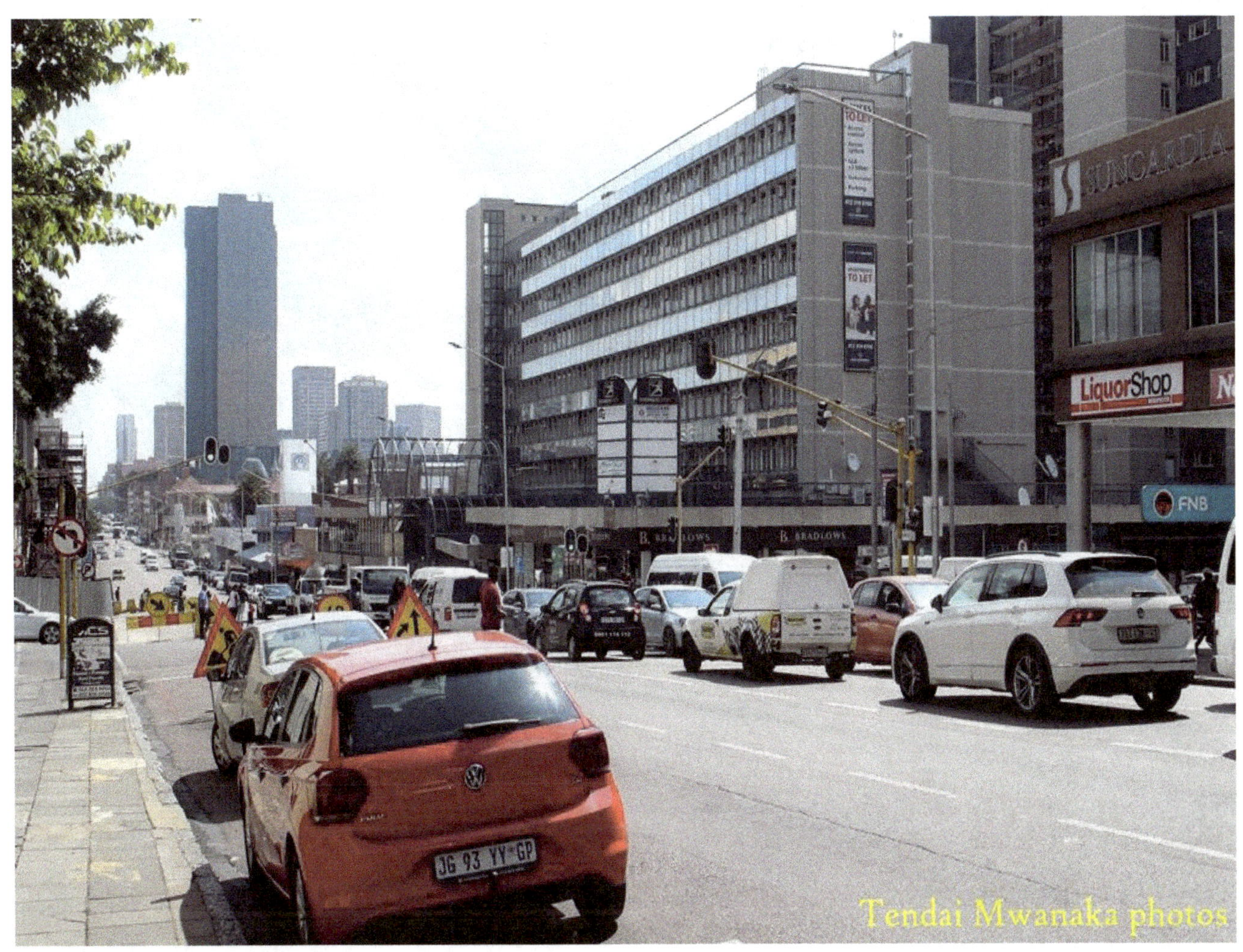

Lining in
2022

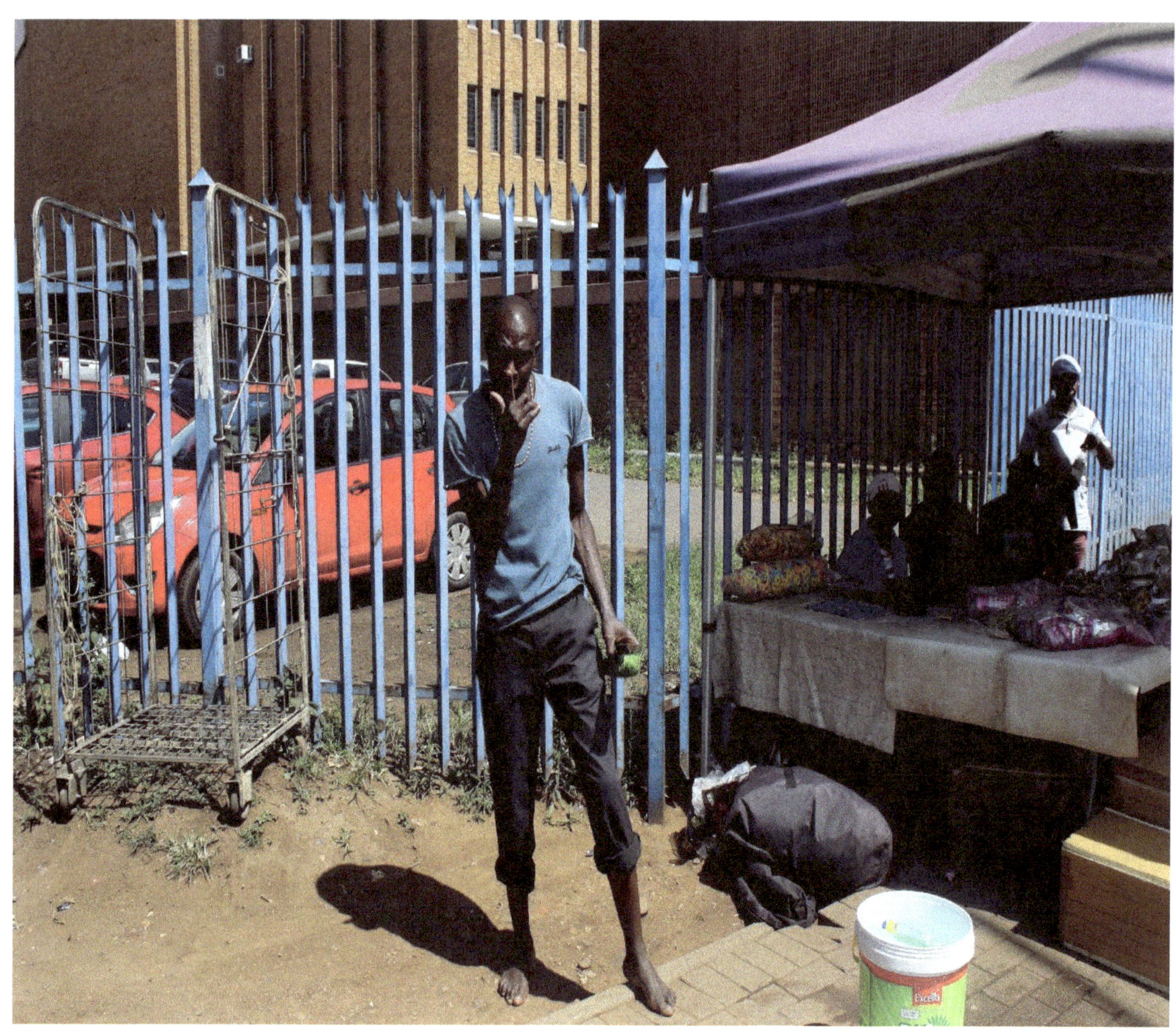

Watch out!
2022

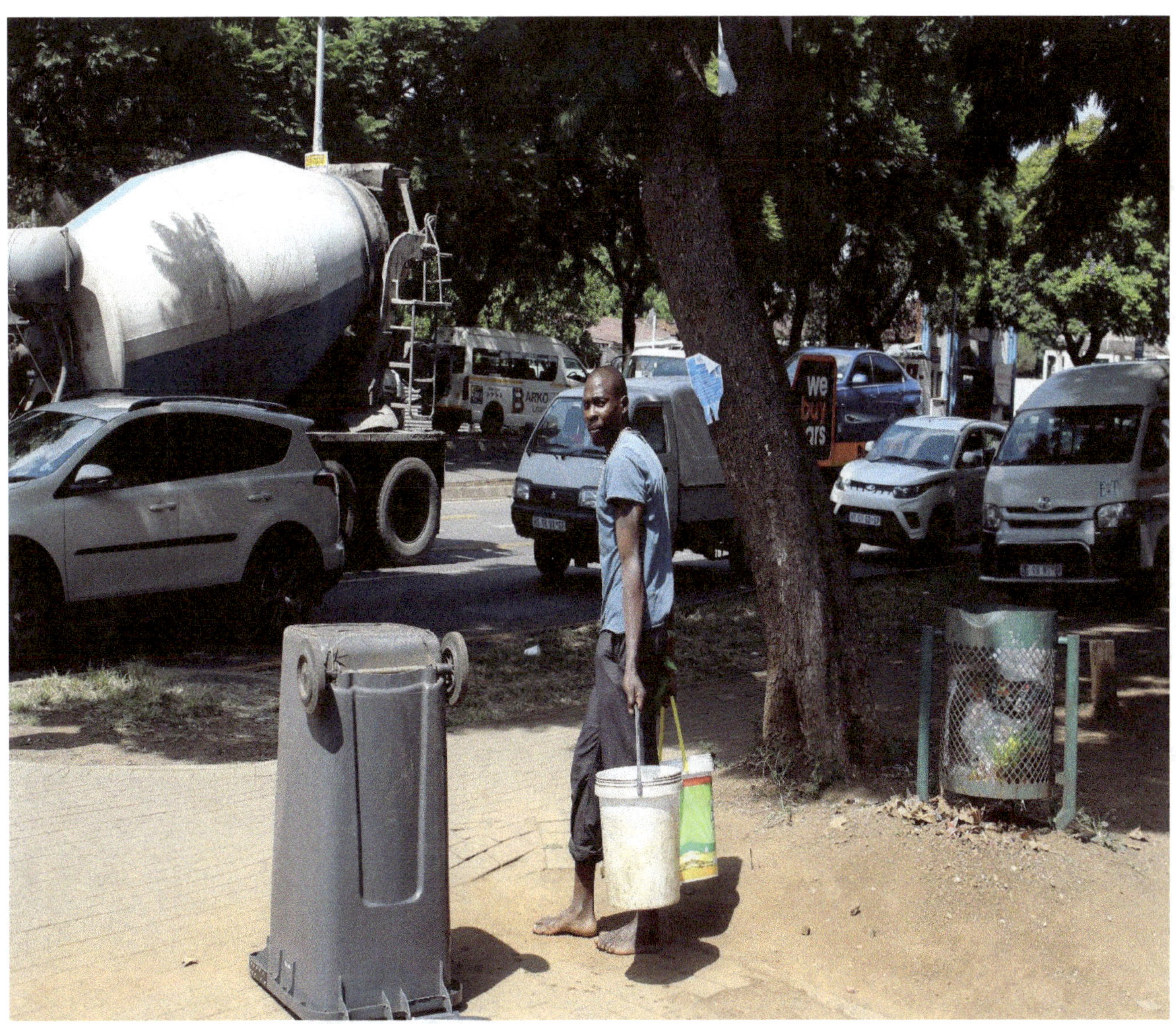

Water crisis
2022

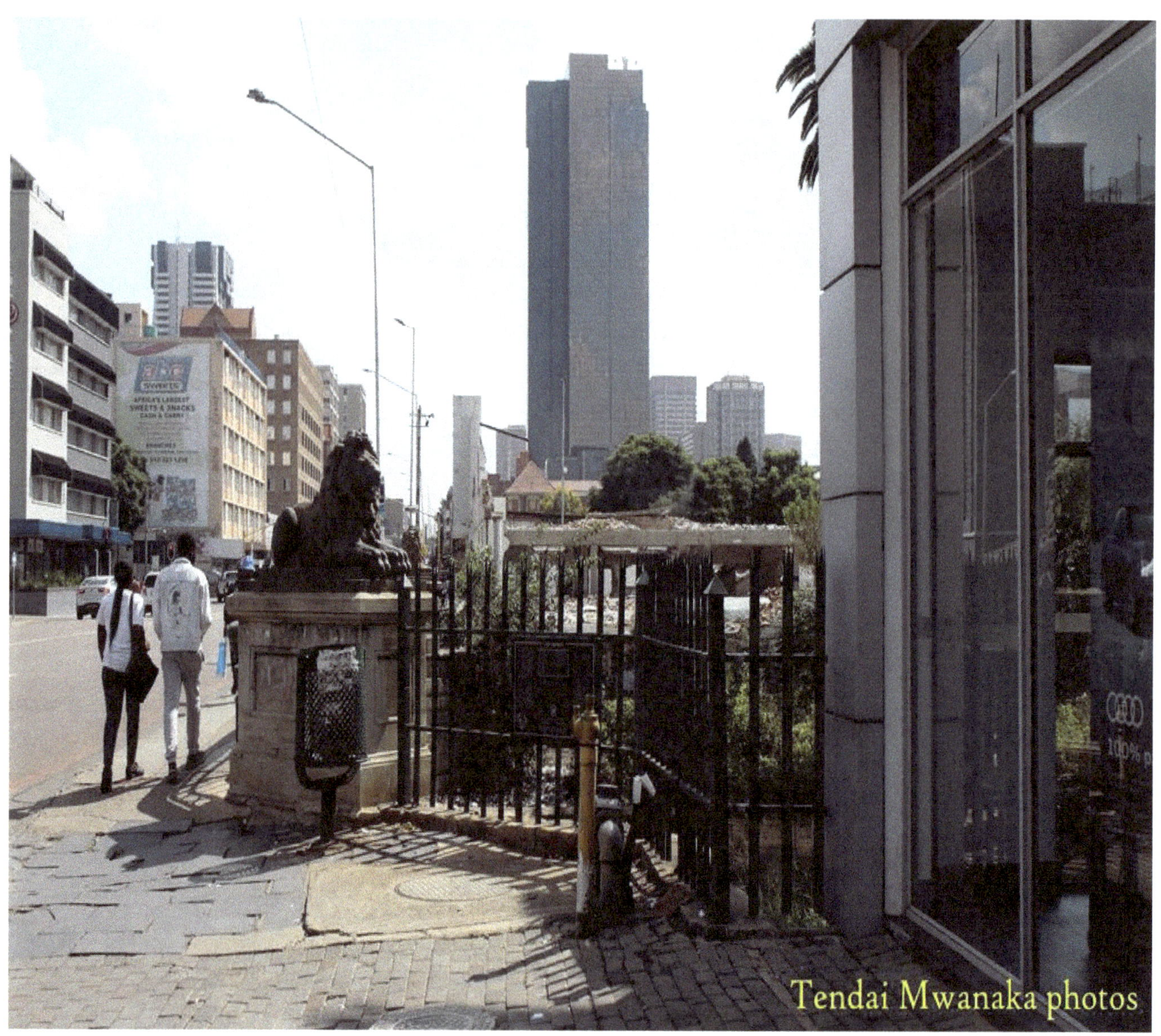

The Lion's bridge
2022

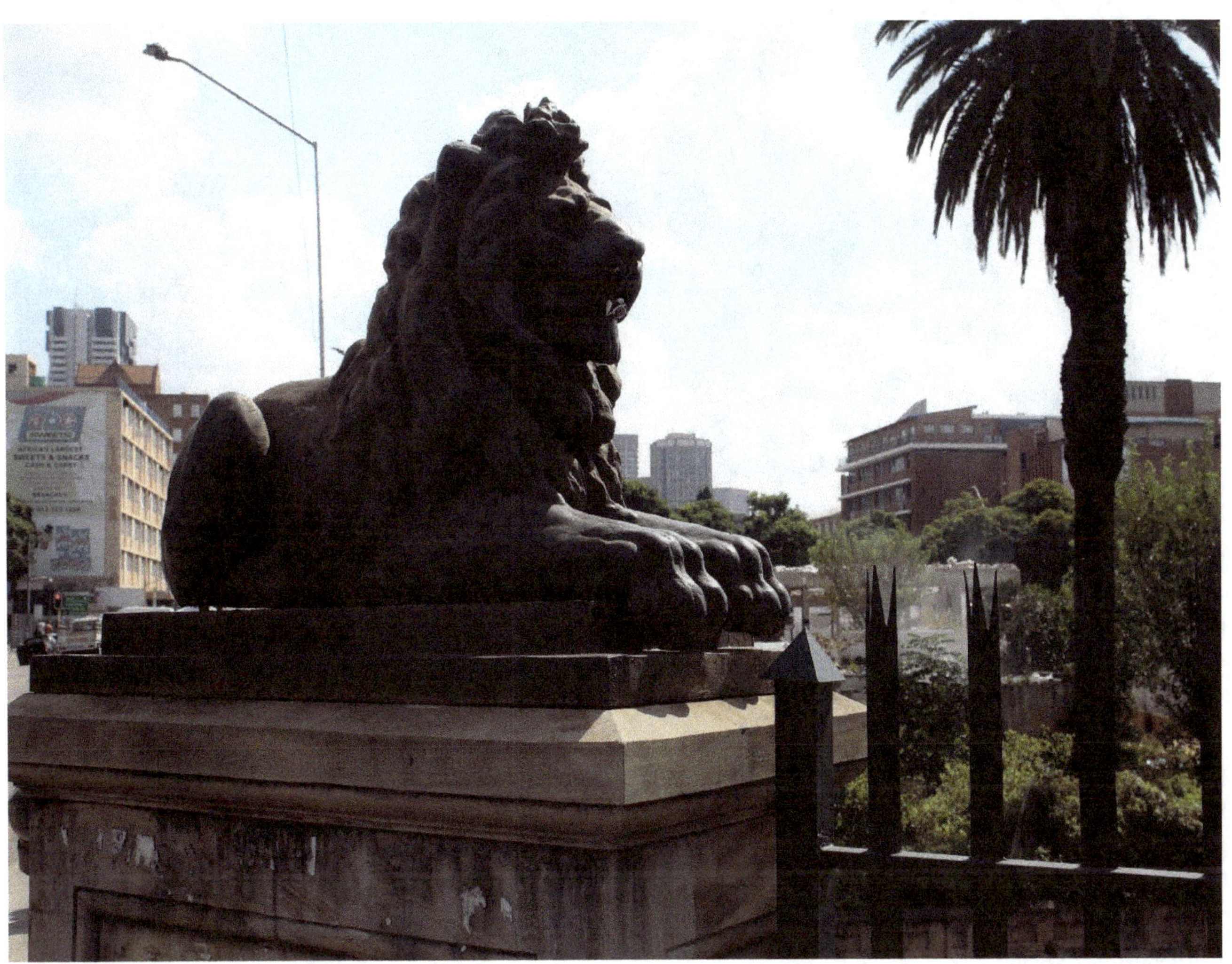

Master of the Concrete Jungle
2022

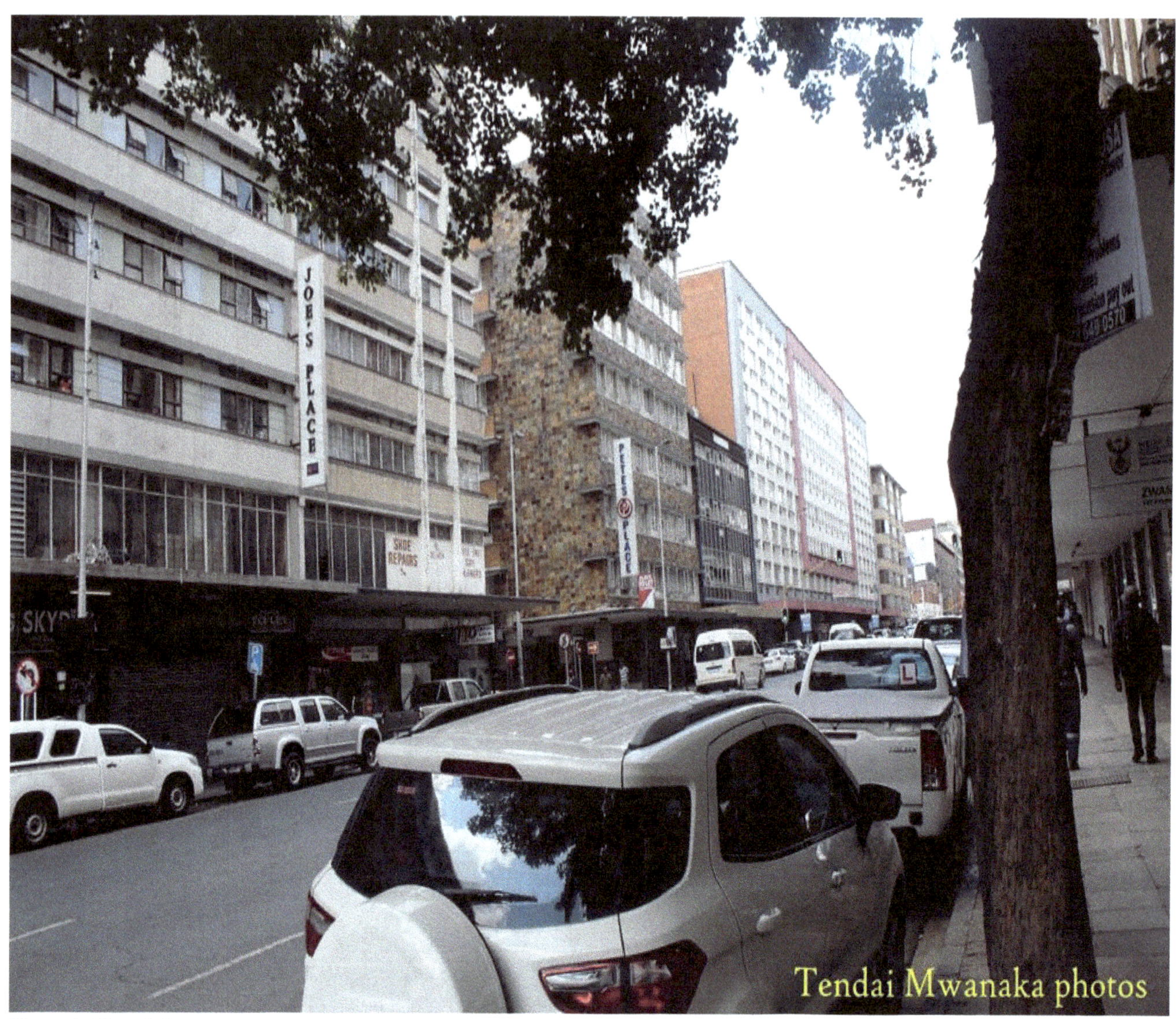

Francis Baad Street
2022

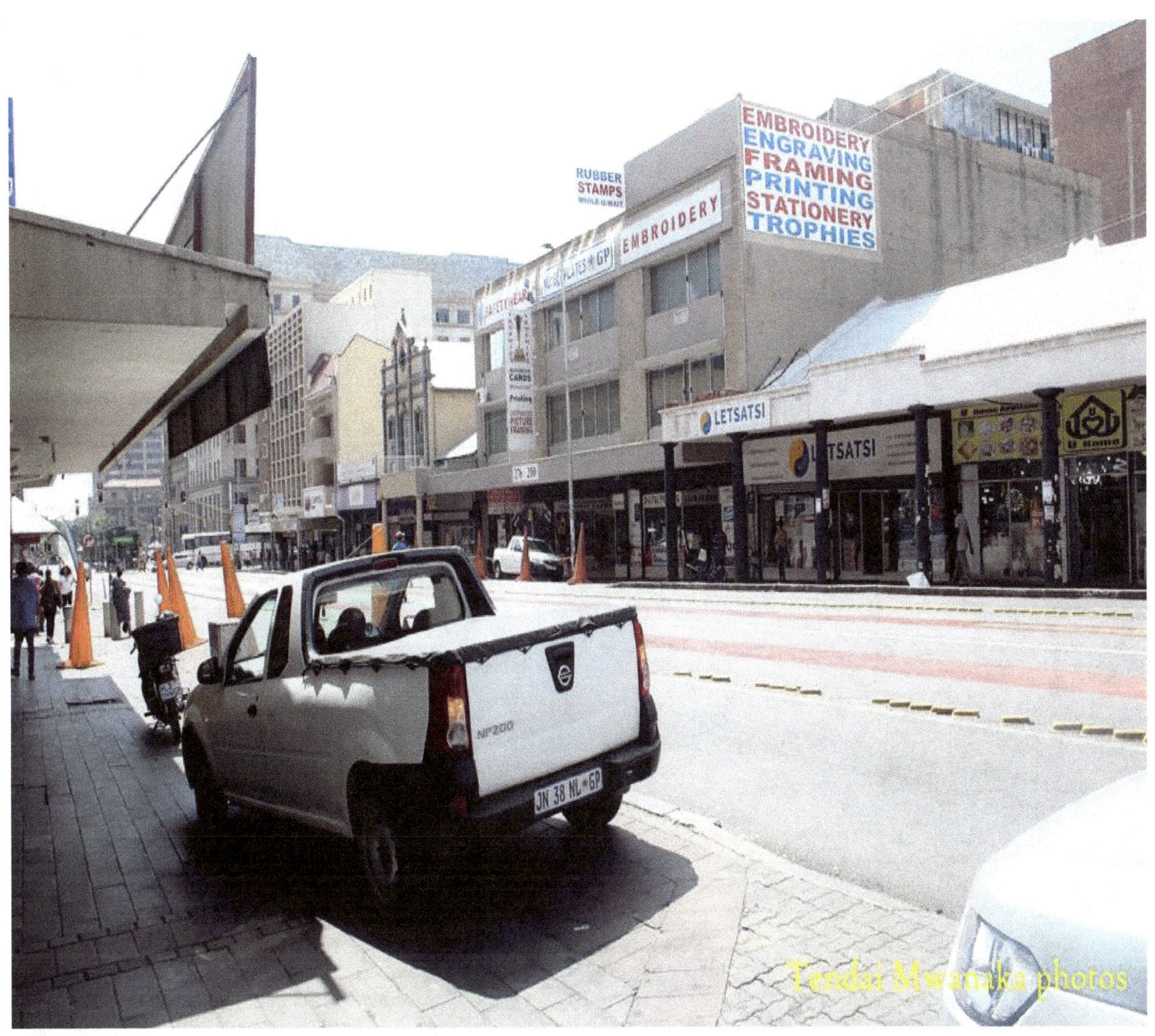

Angular
2022

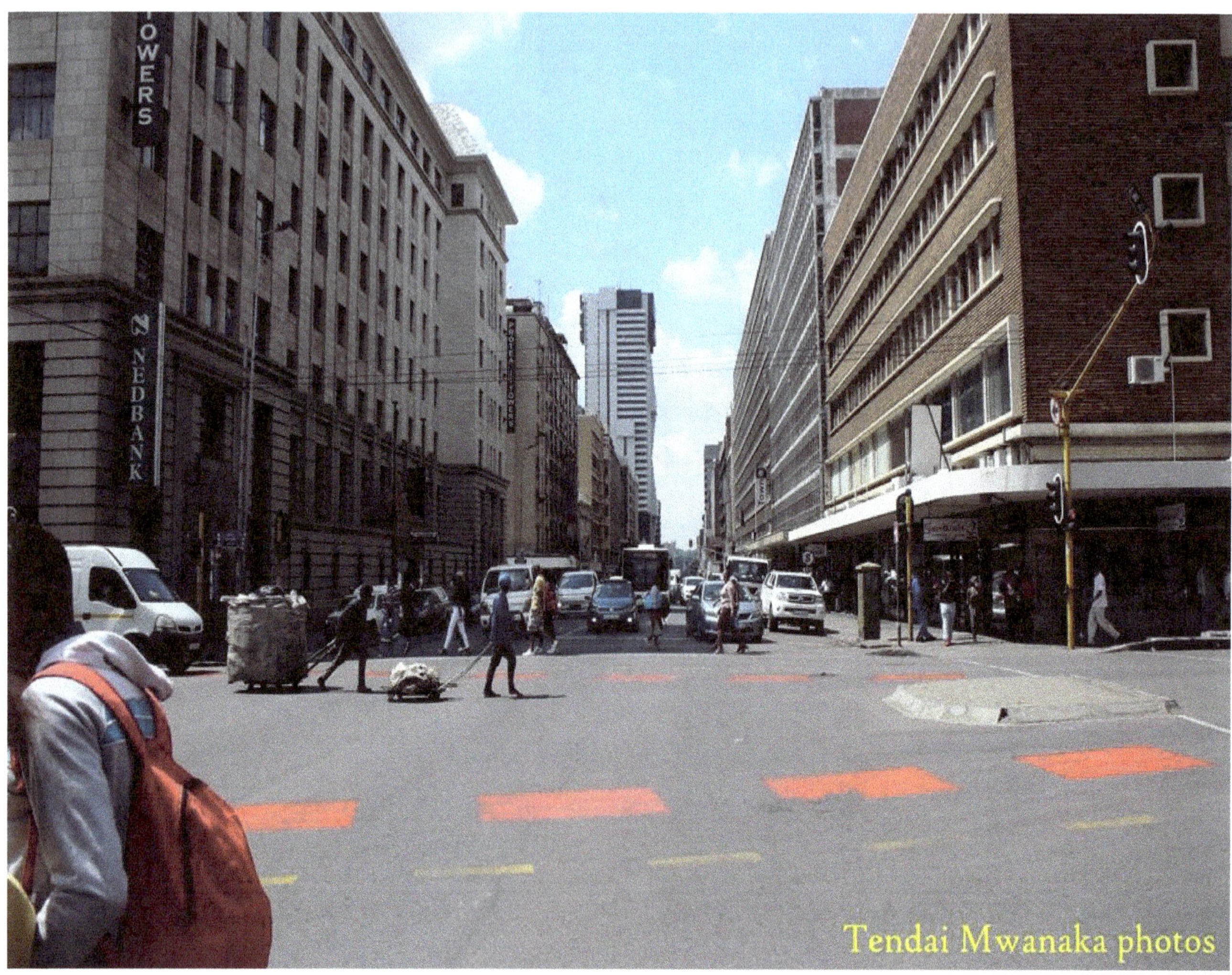

Pull lines
2022

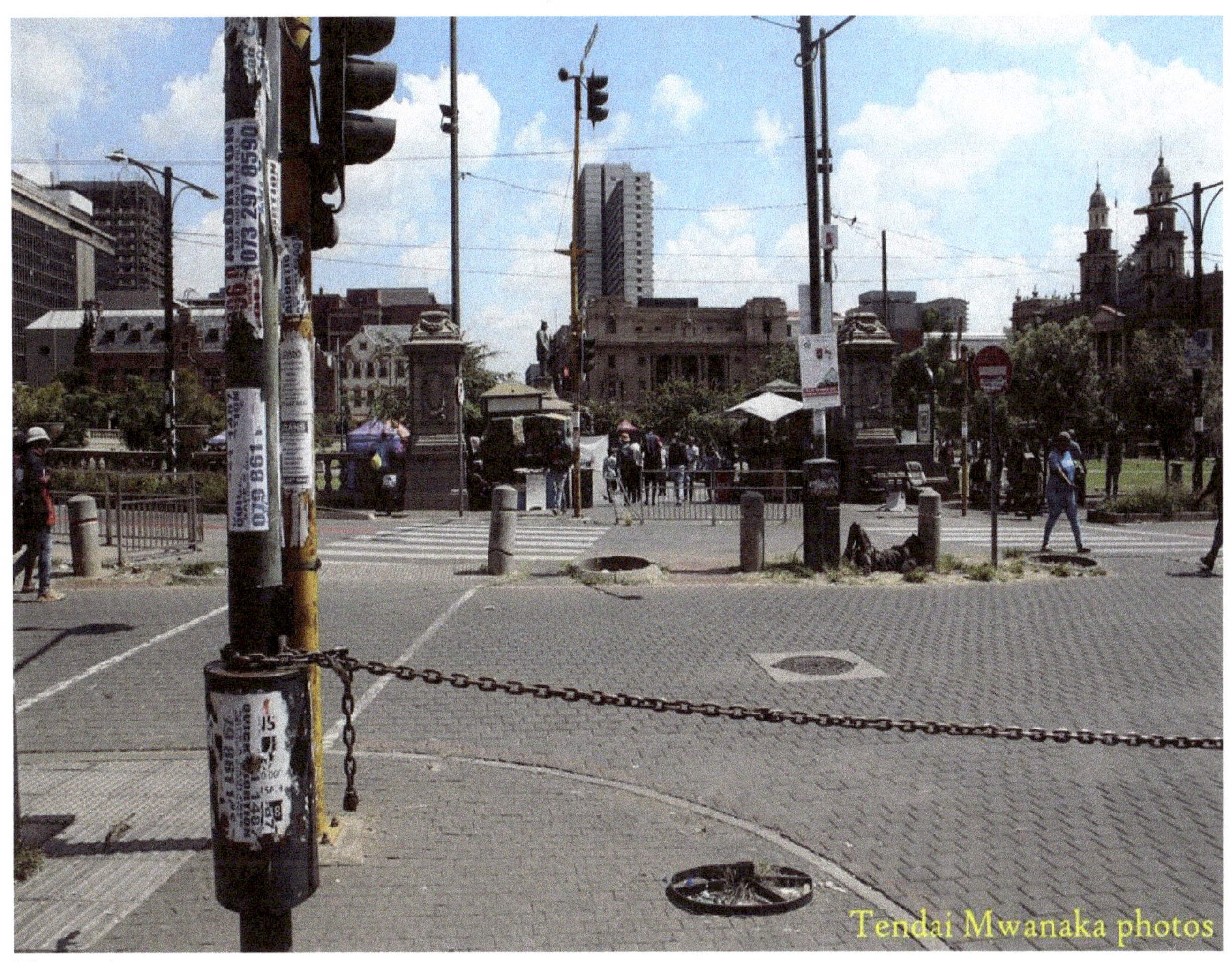

No way in
2022

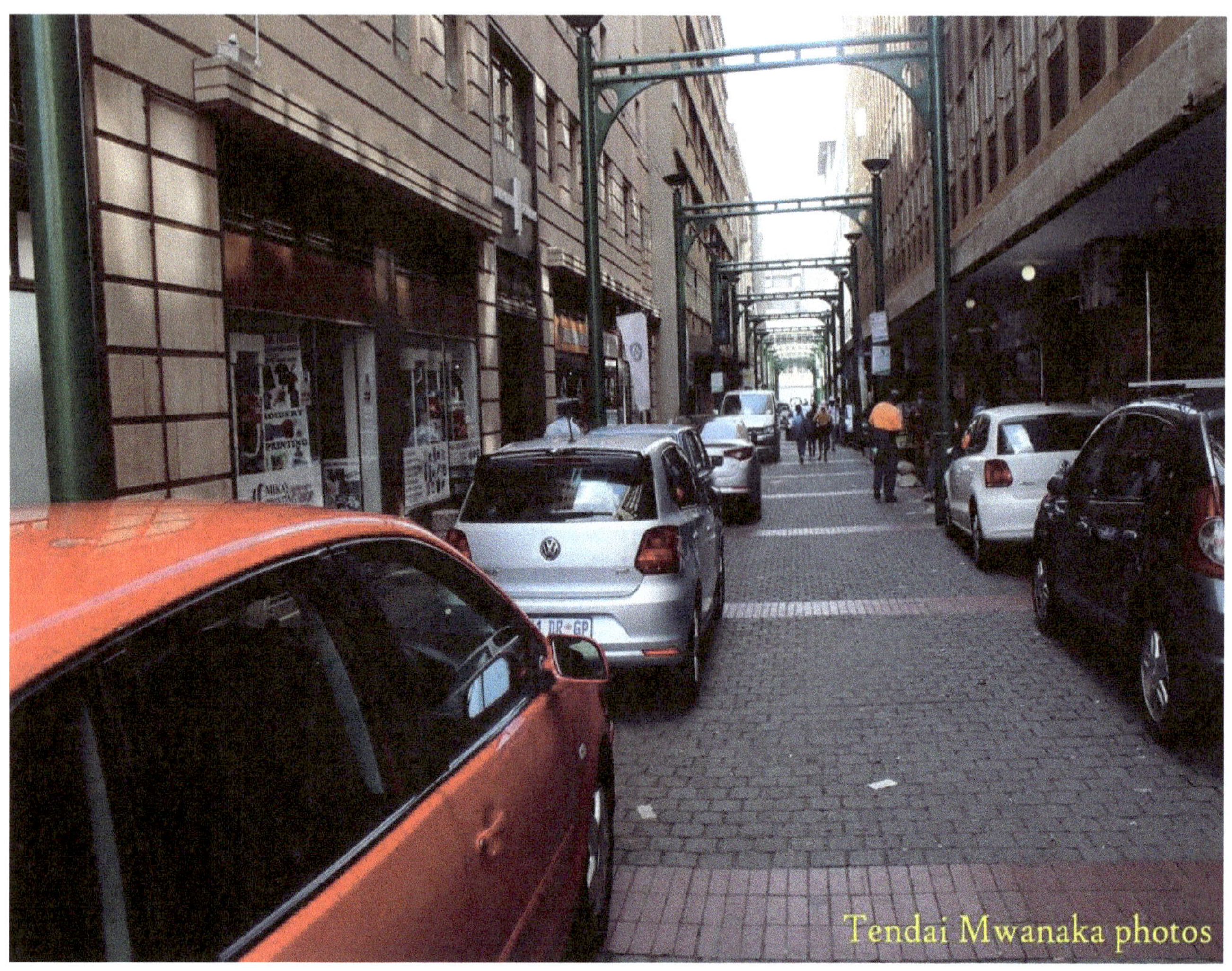

Contained
2022

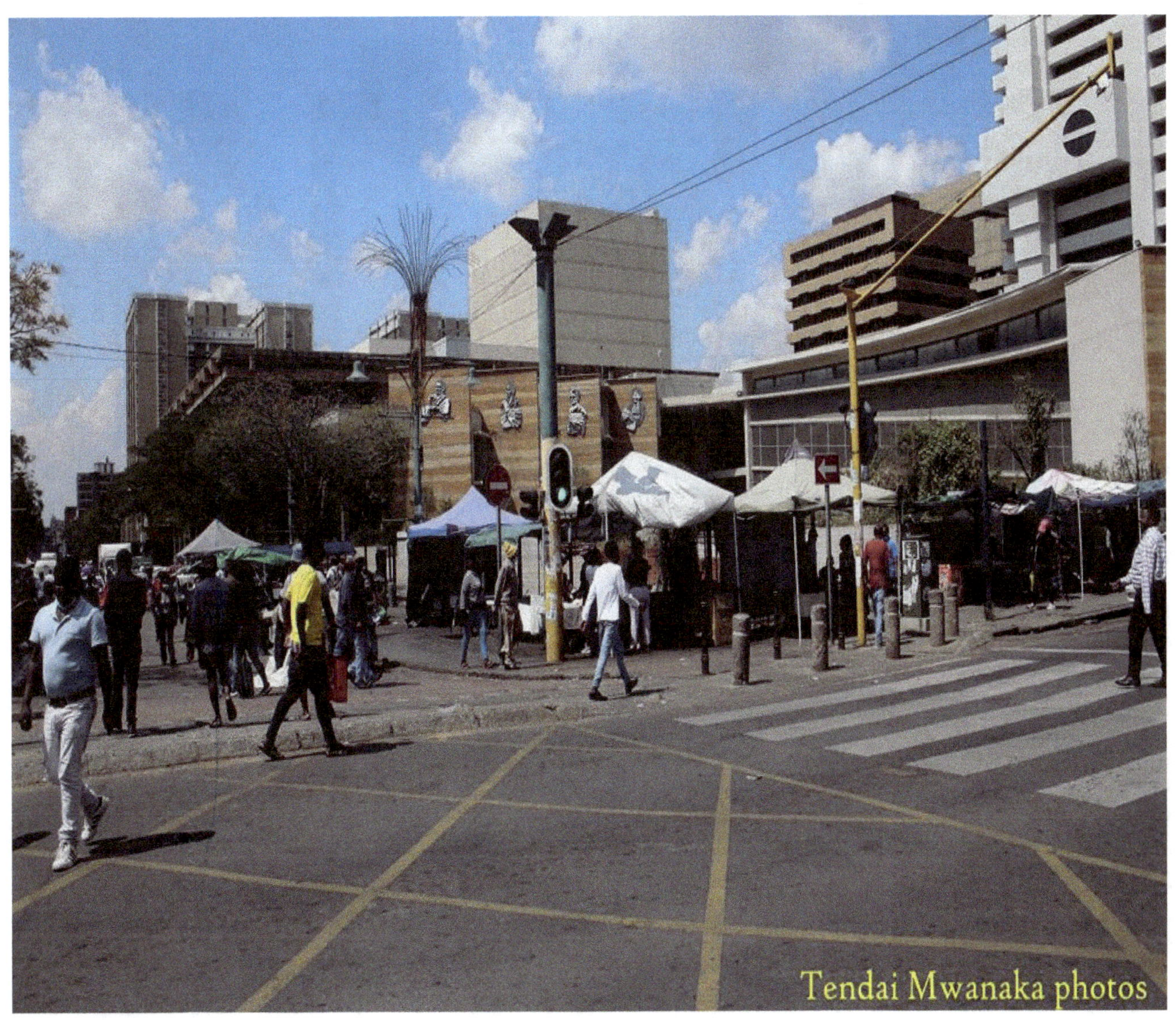

Chessboard
2022

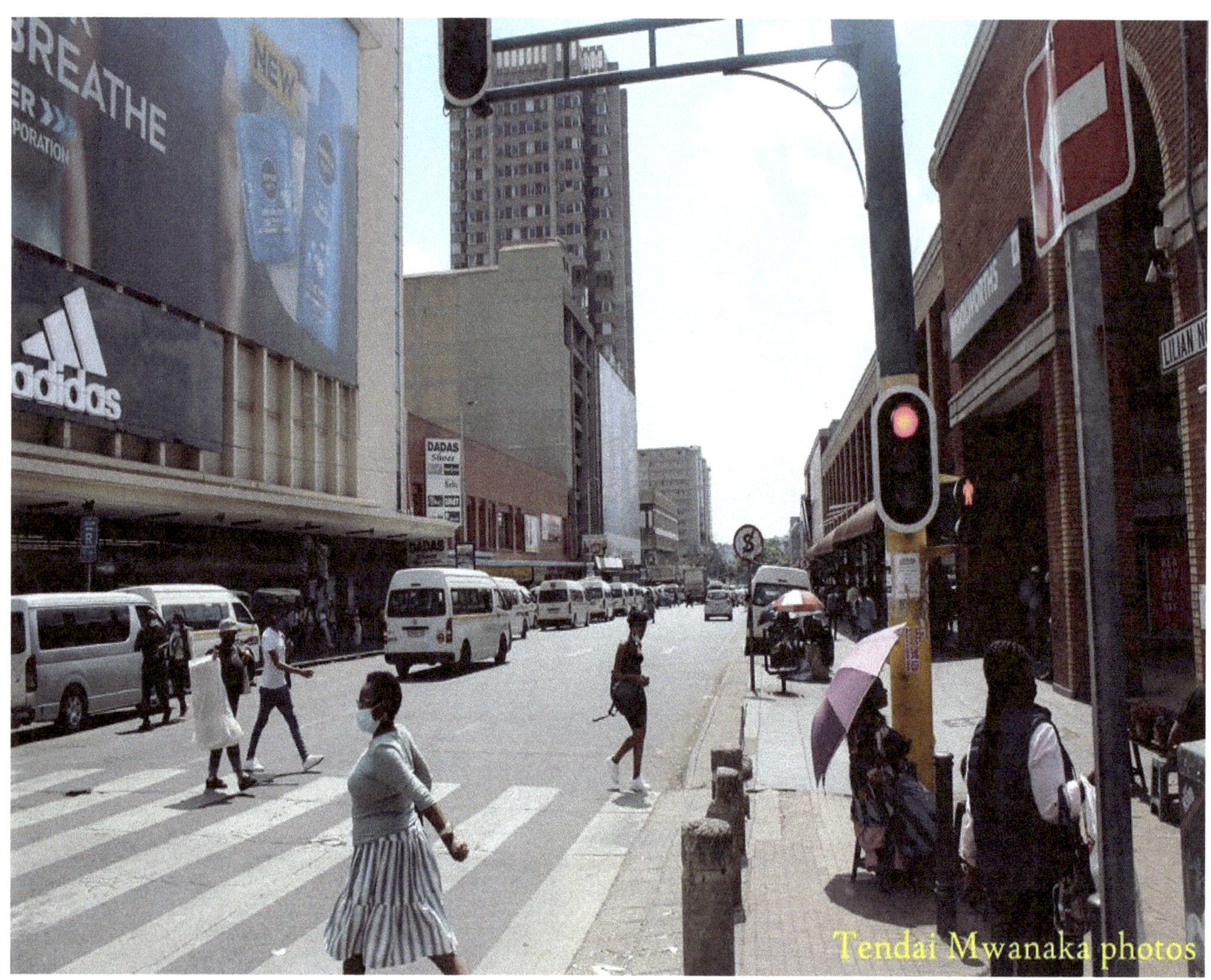

Walking the Lillian Ngoyi way
2022

VISUAL ART

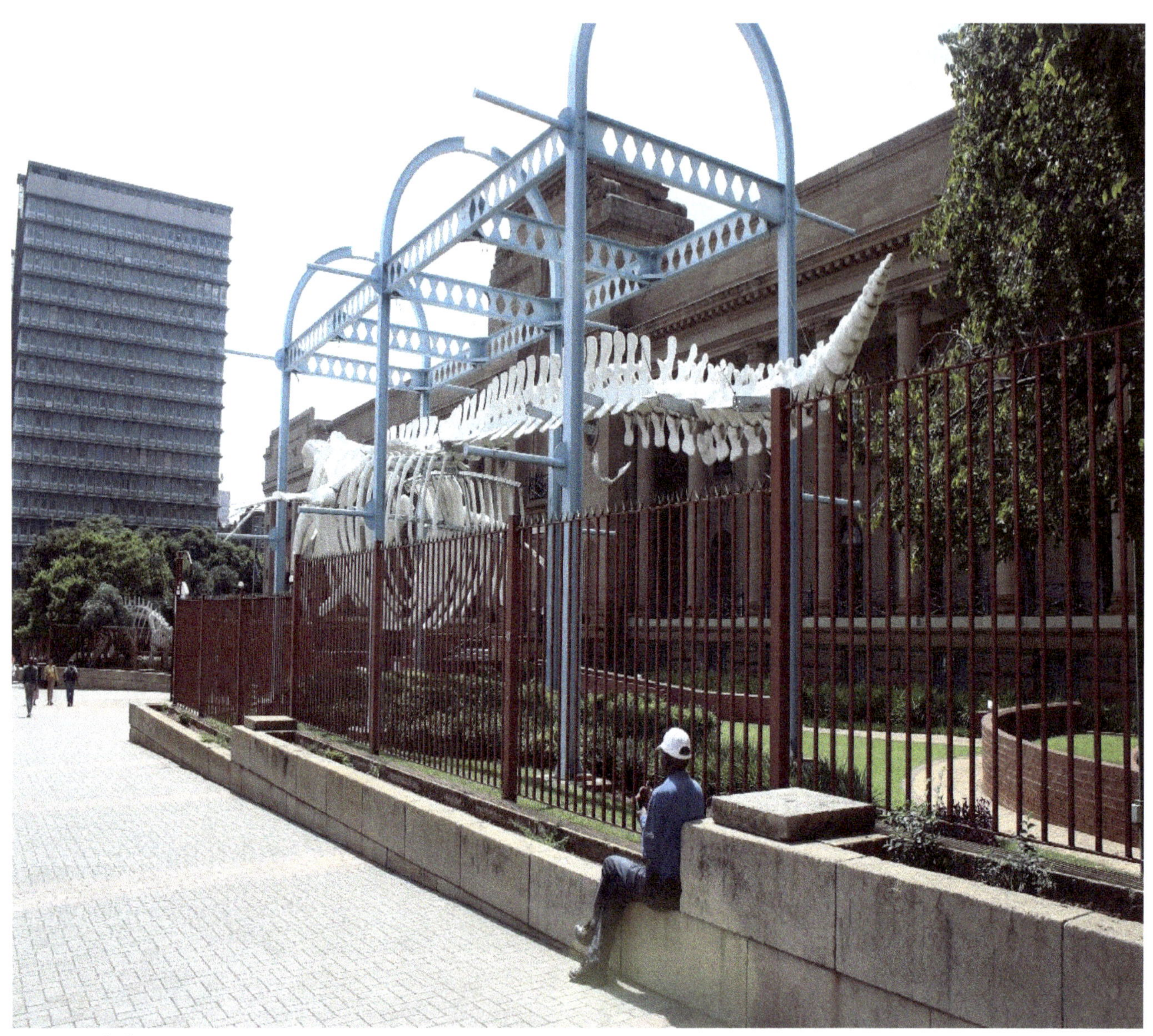

Big Rex leftovers
2022

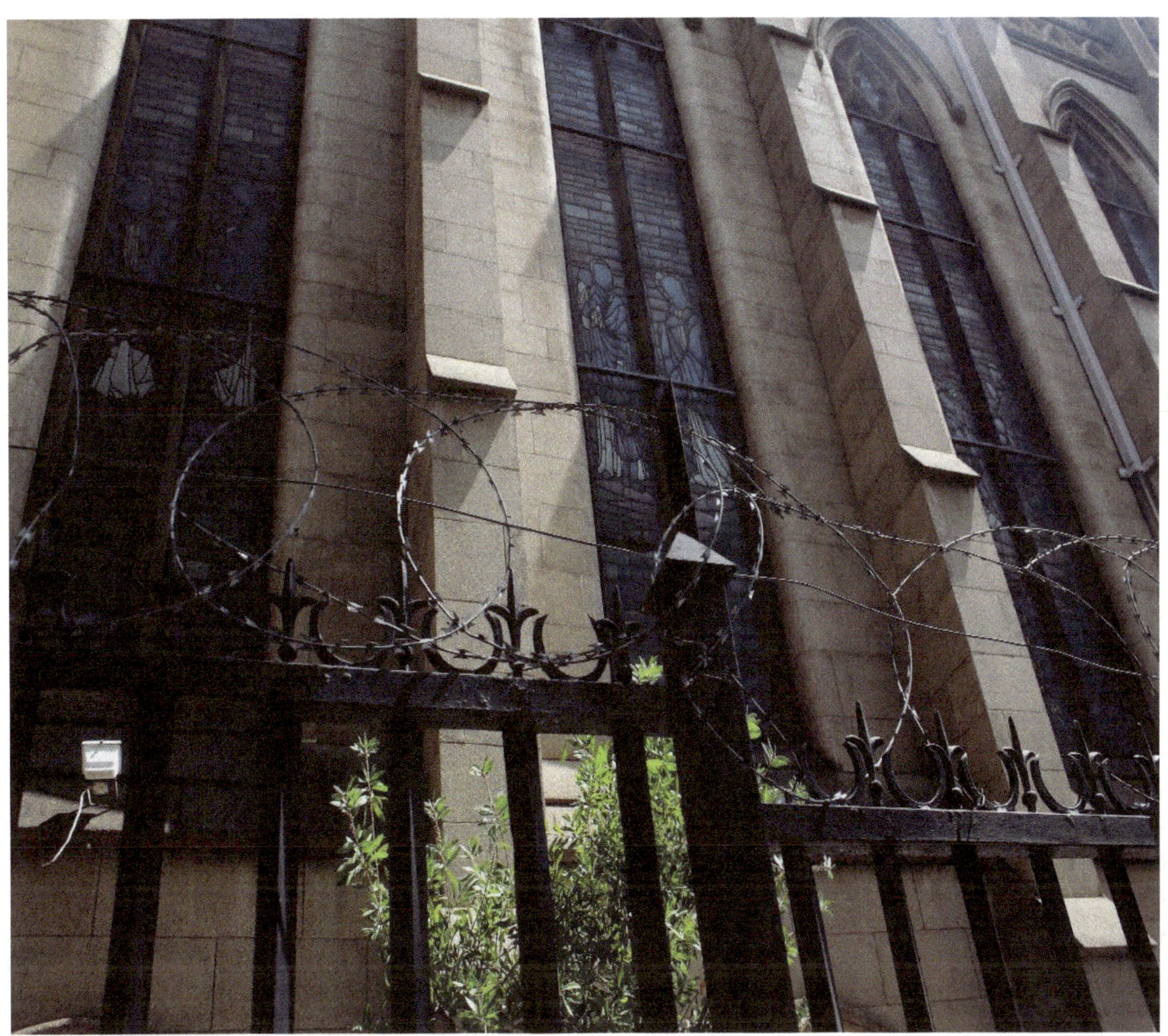

Catholic Cathedral frescoes
2022

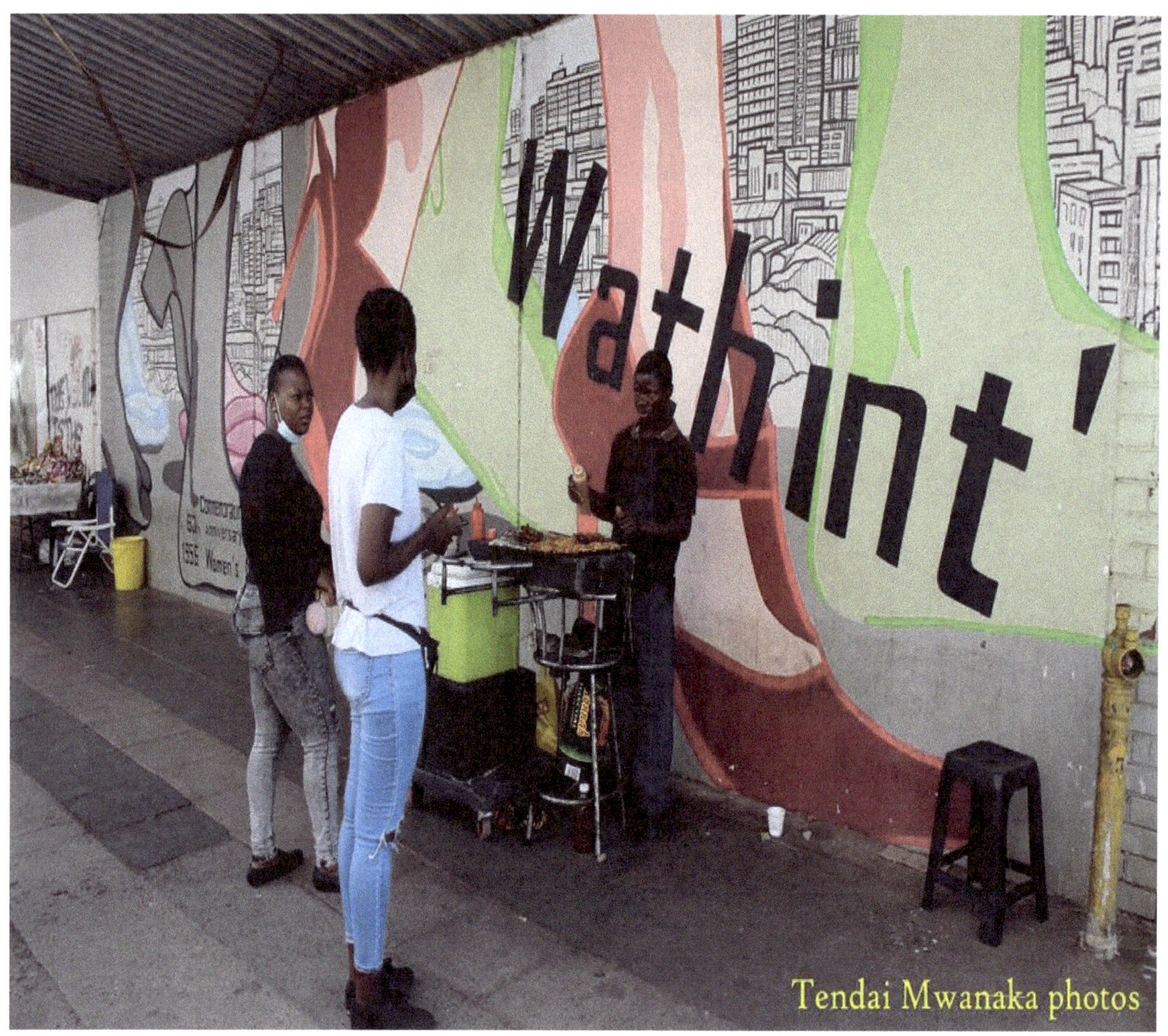

Open exhibition: Food and Art
2022

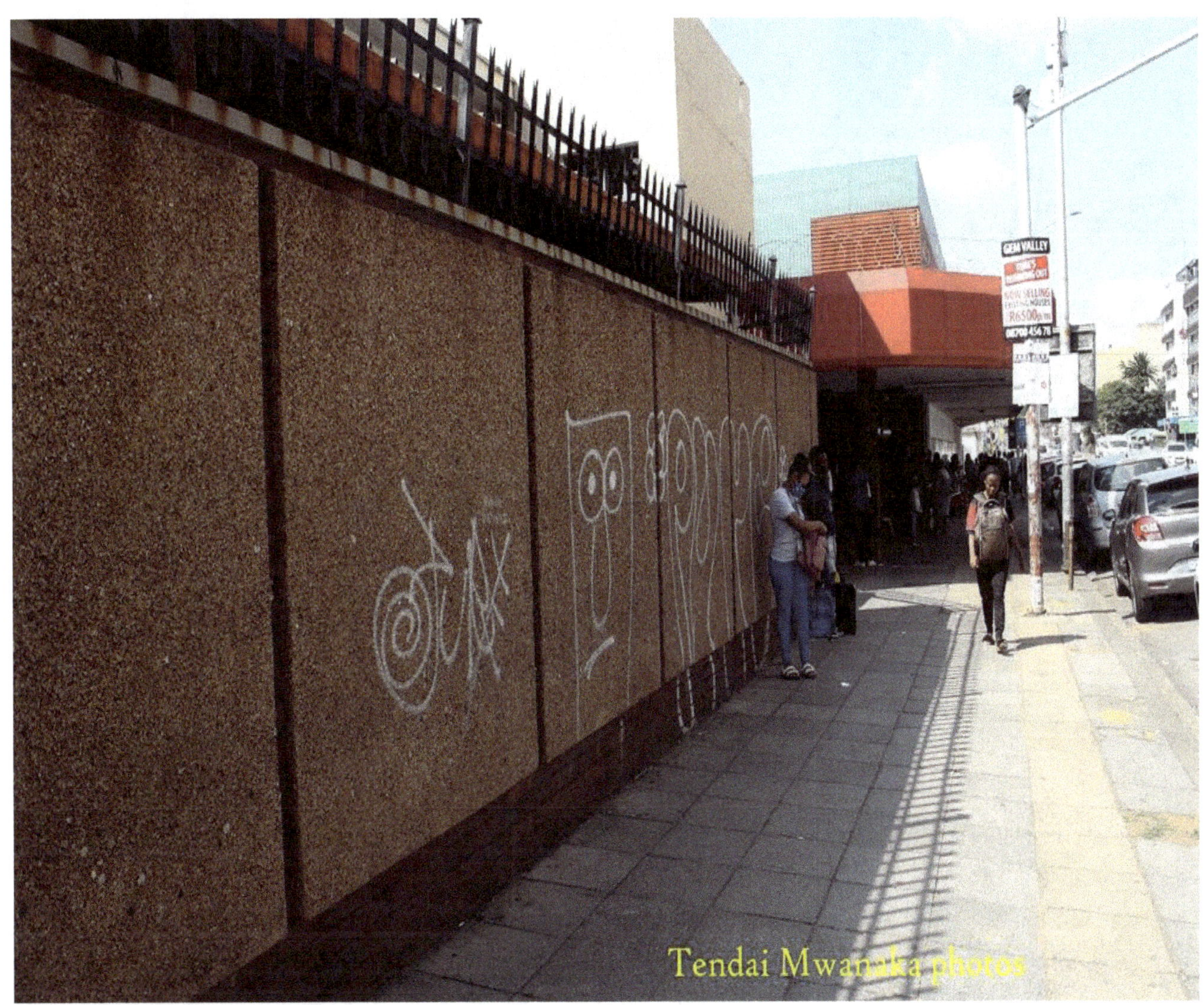

Street exhibition: human noises
2022

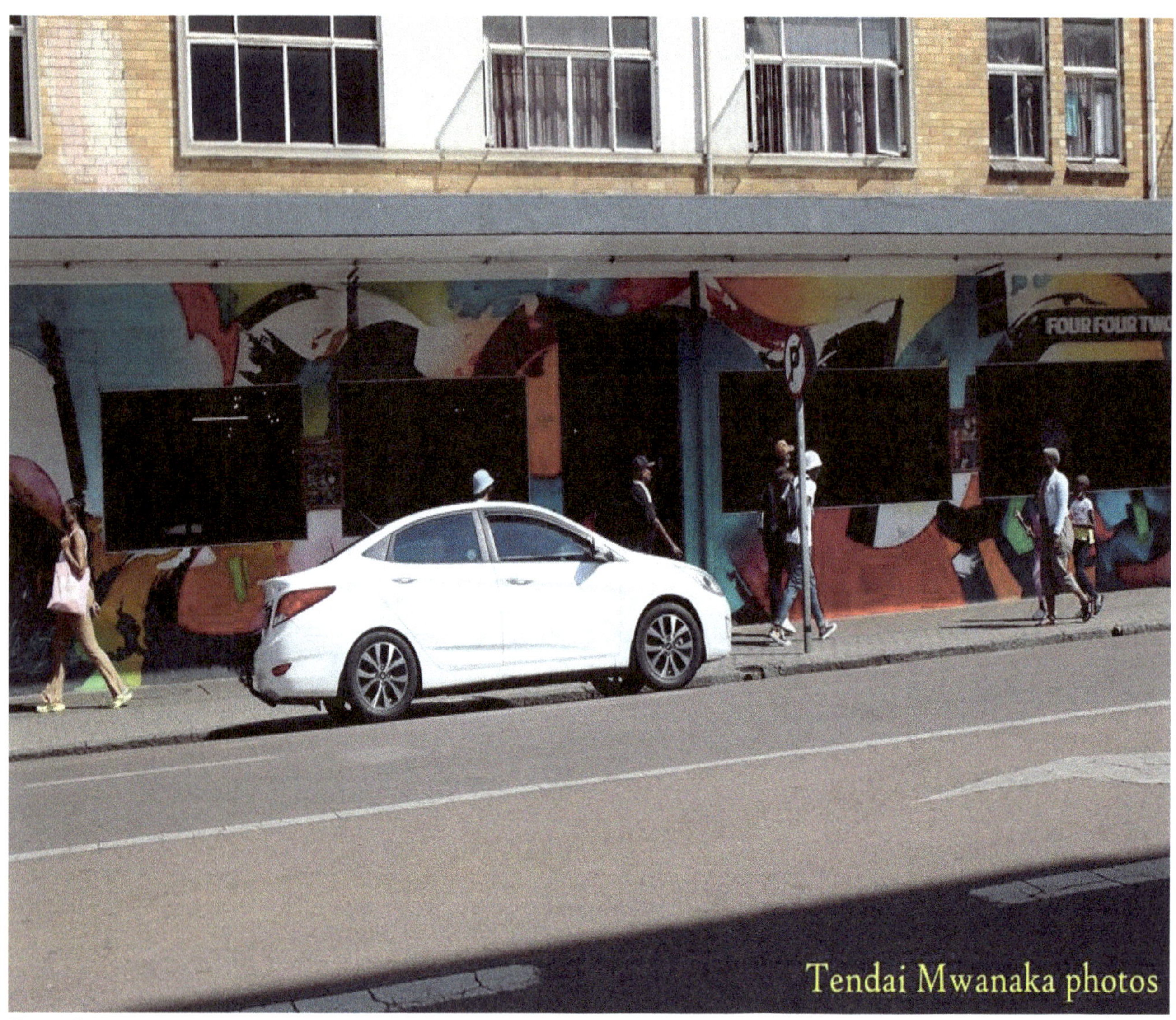

Four four two
2022

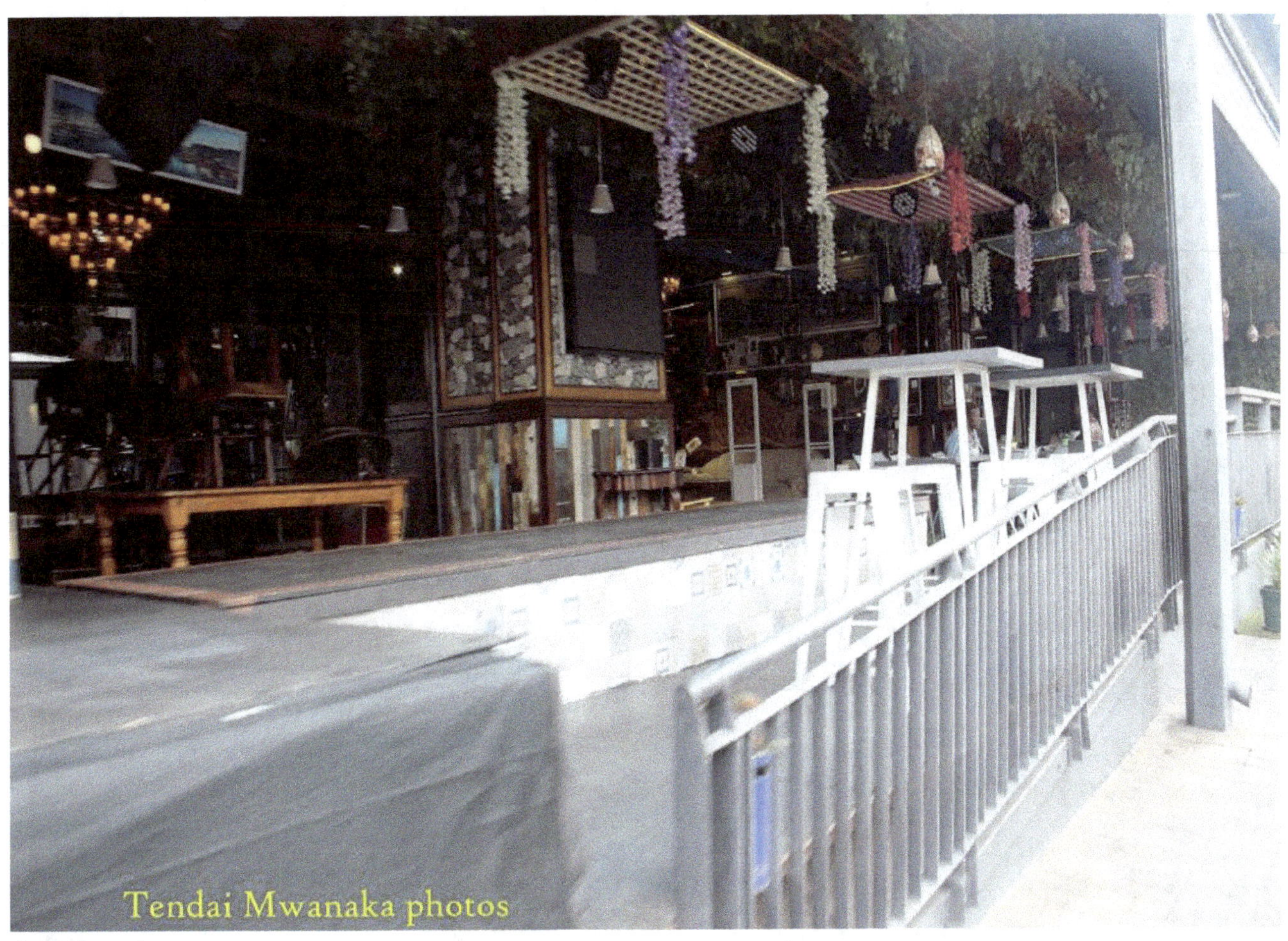

Arty, hanging...
2022

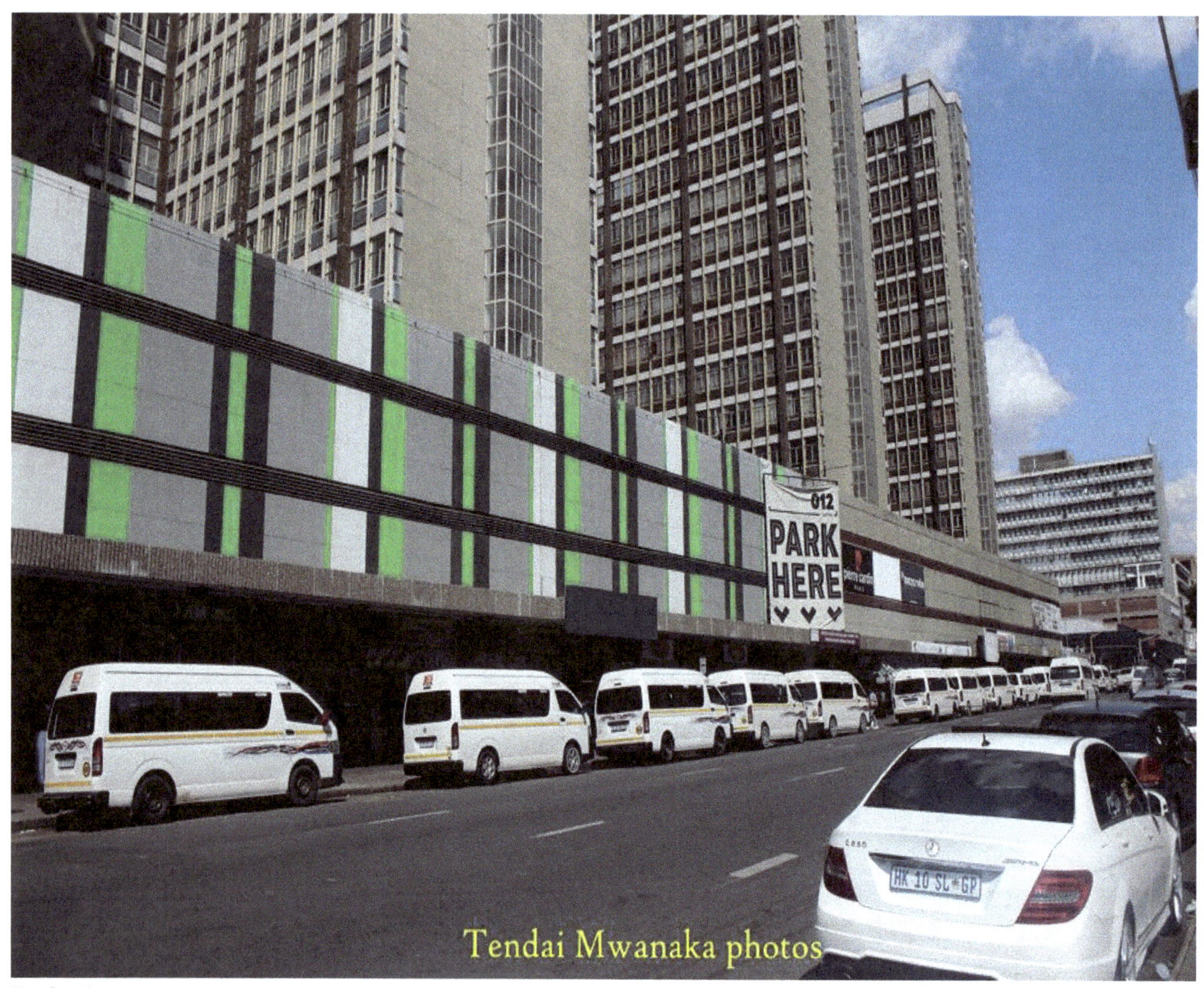

Parked
2022

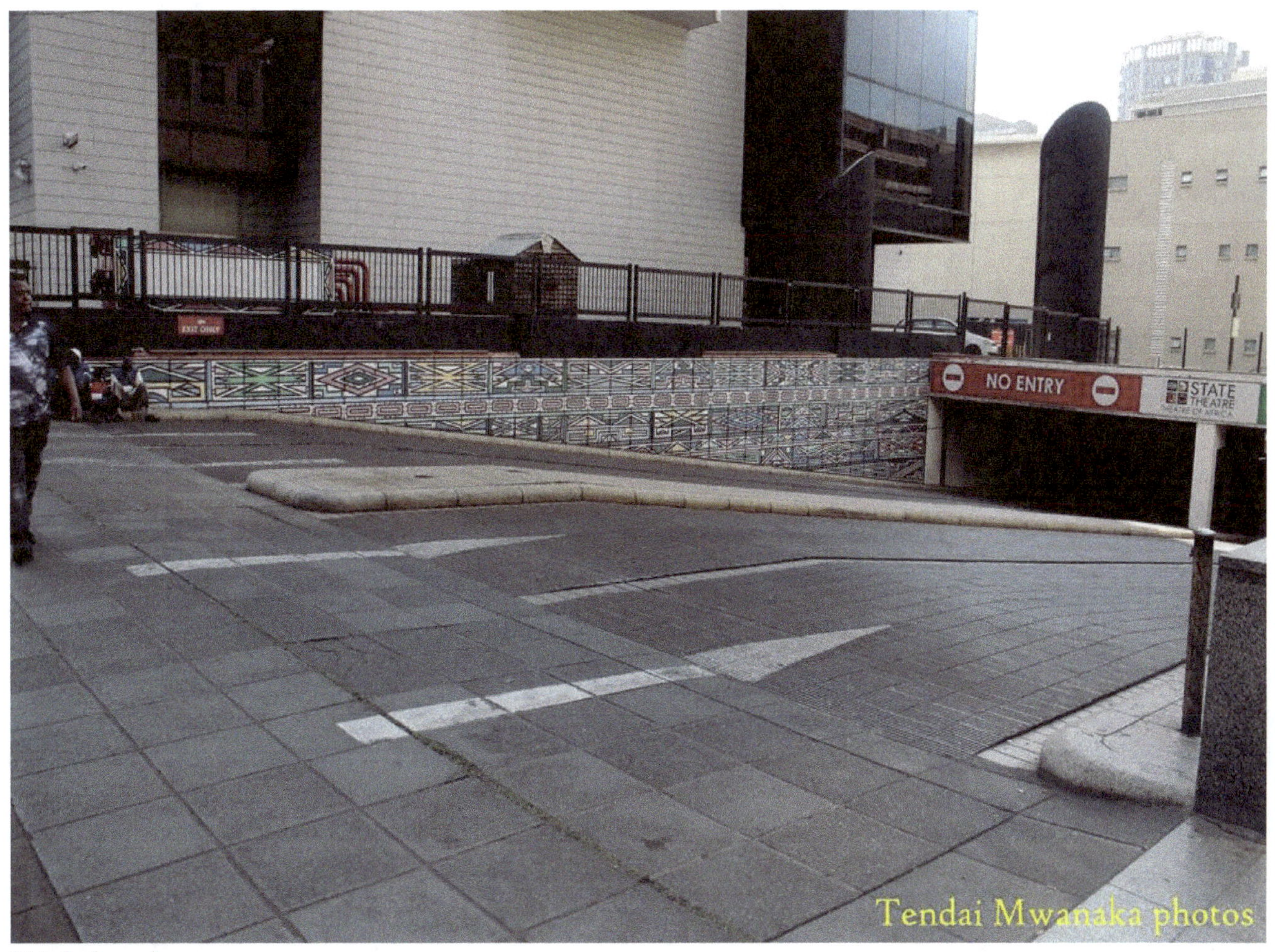

Ndebele colours
2022

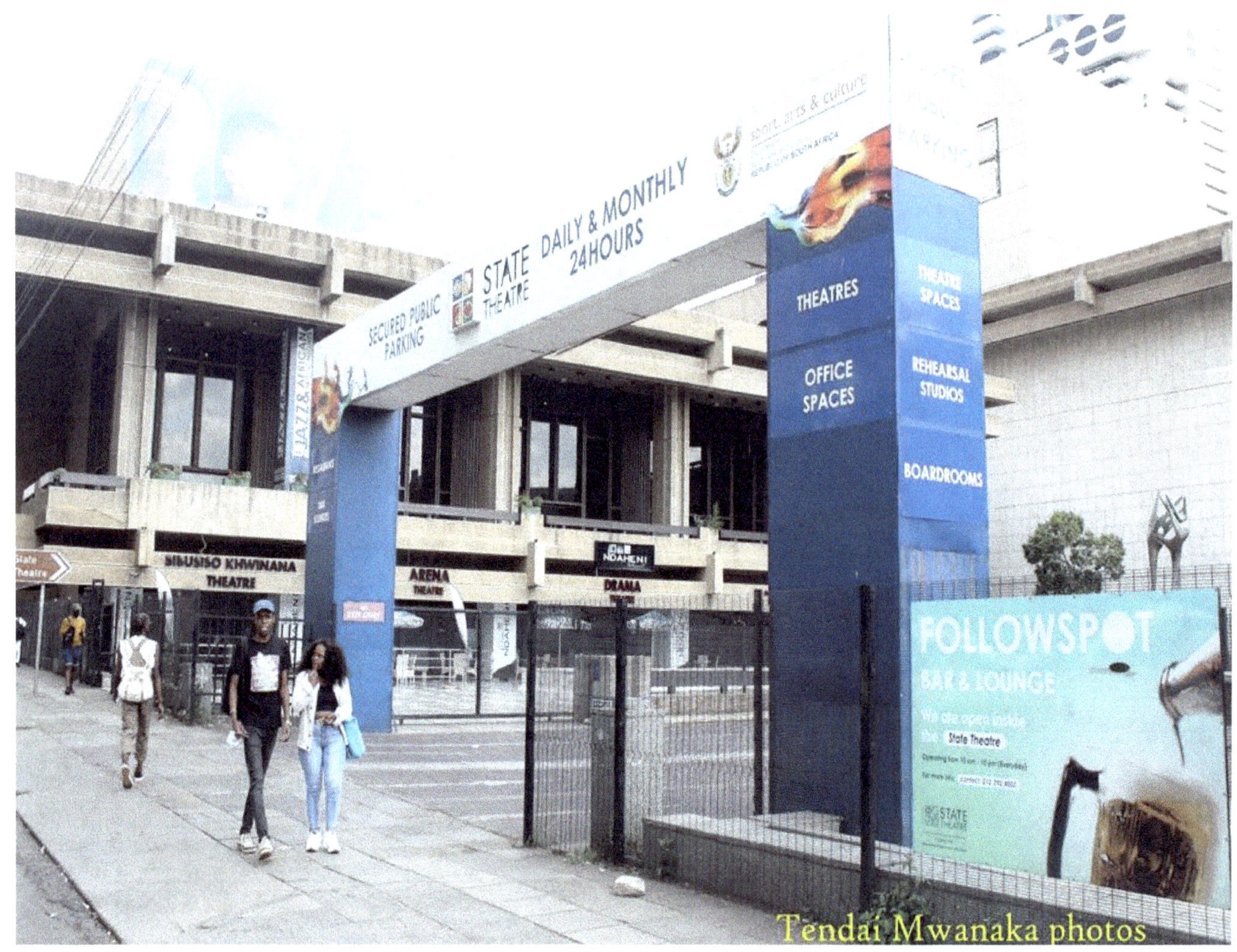

State theatre
2022

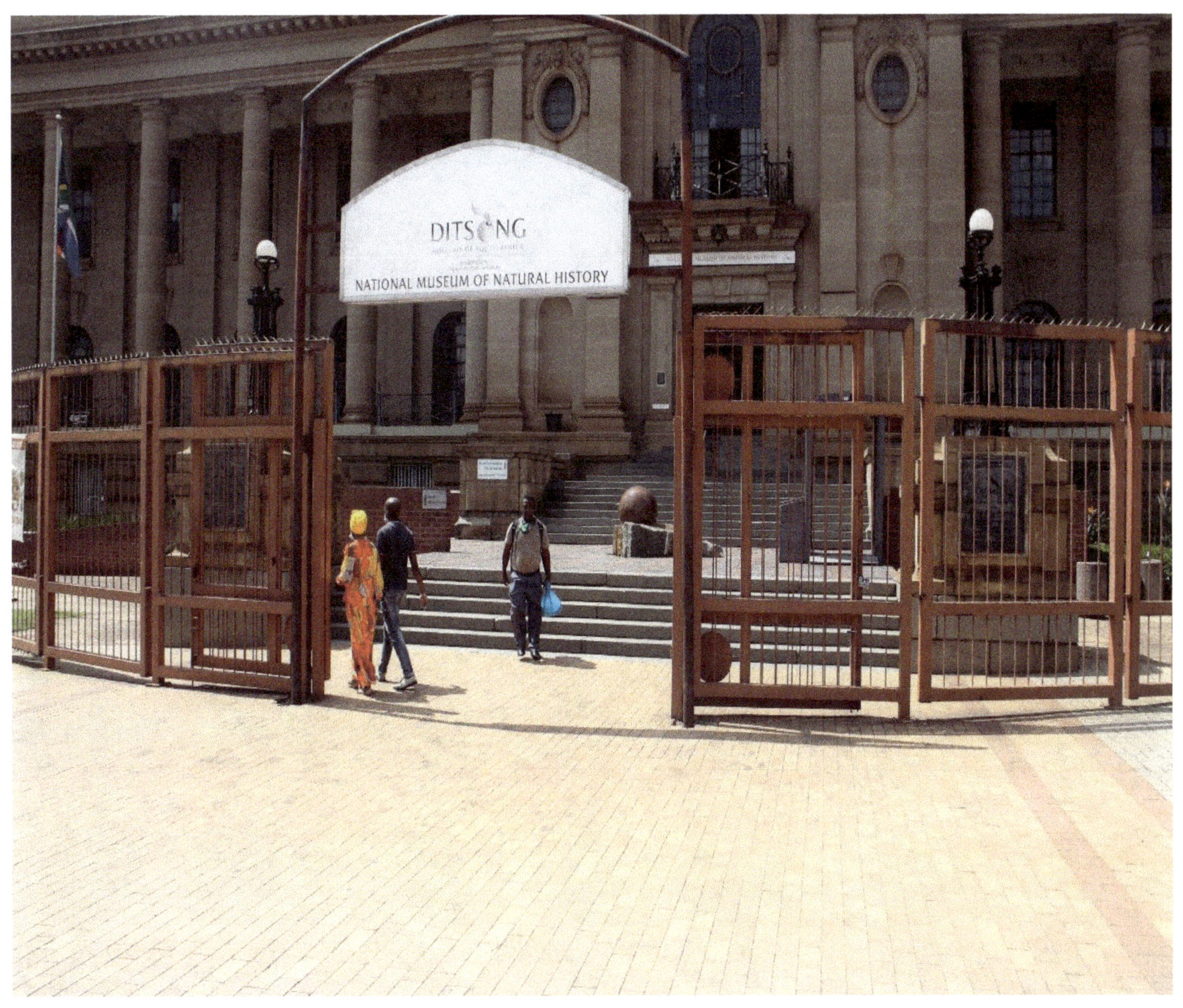

National Museum of Natural History
2022

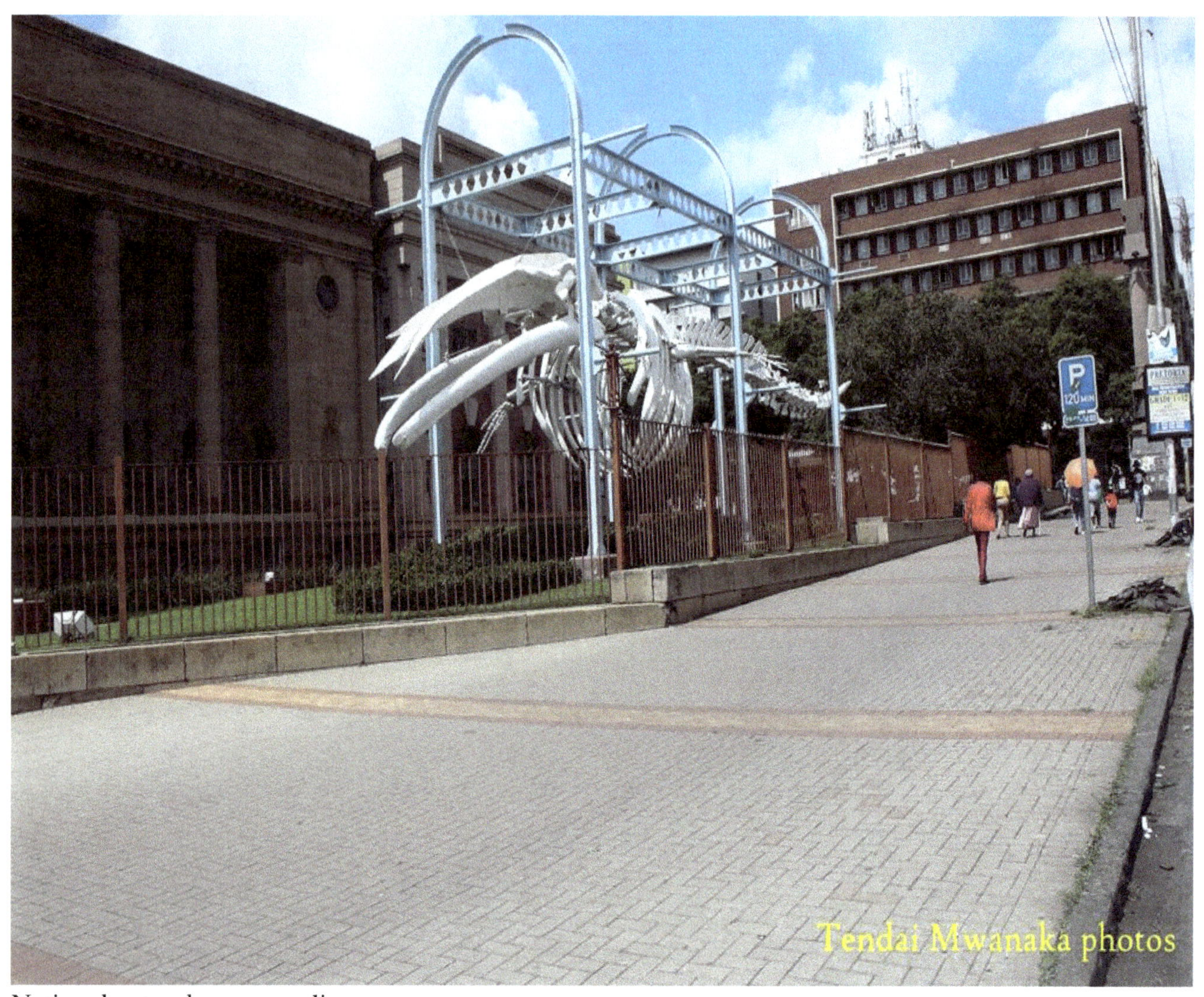

National natural museum dinosaur
2022

PARKS AND PARK BENCHES

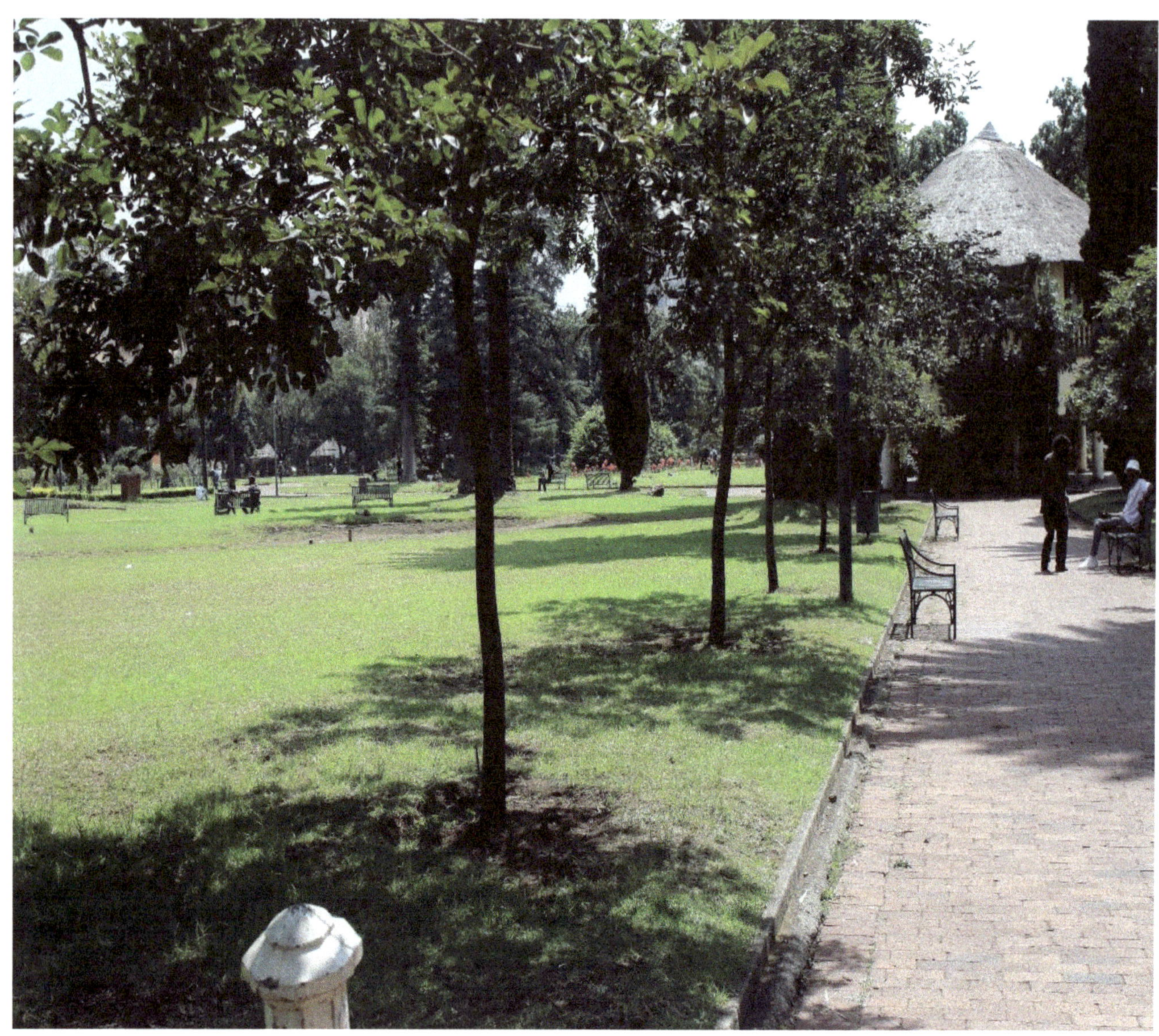

Main entry into Burgers Park
2022

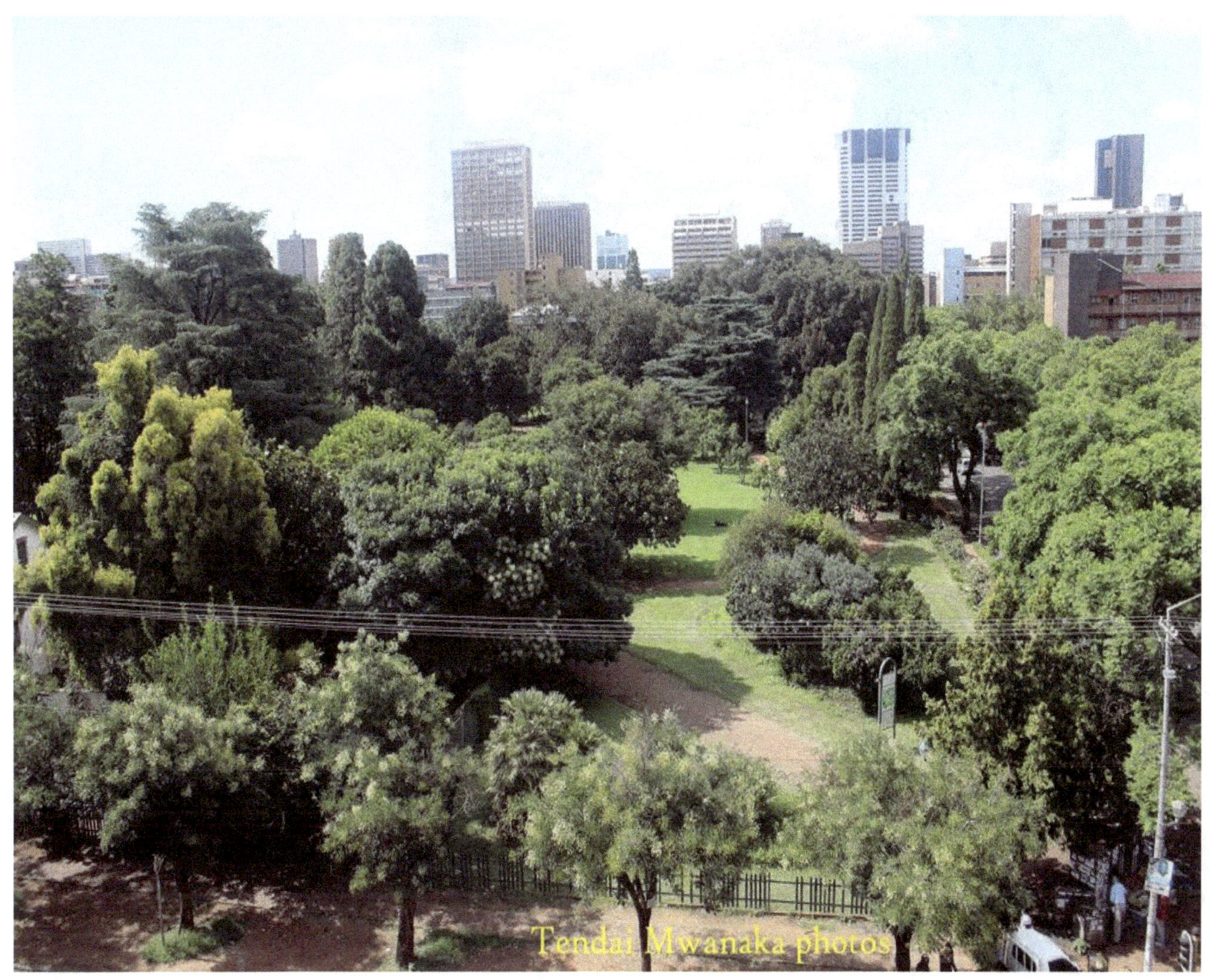

Park dreams
2022

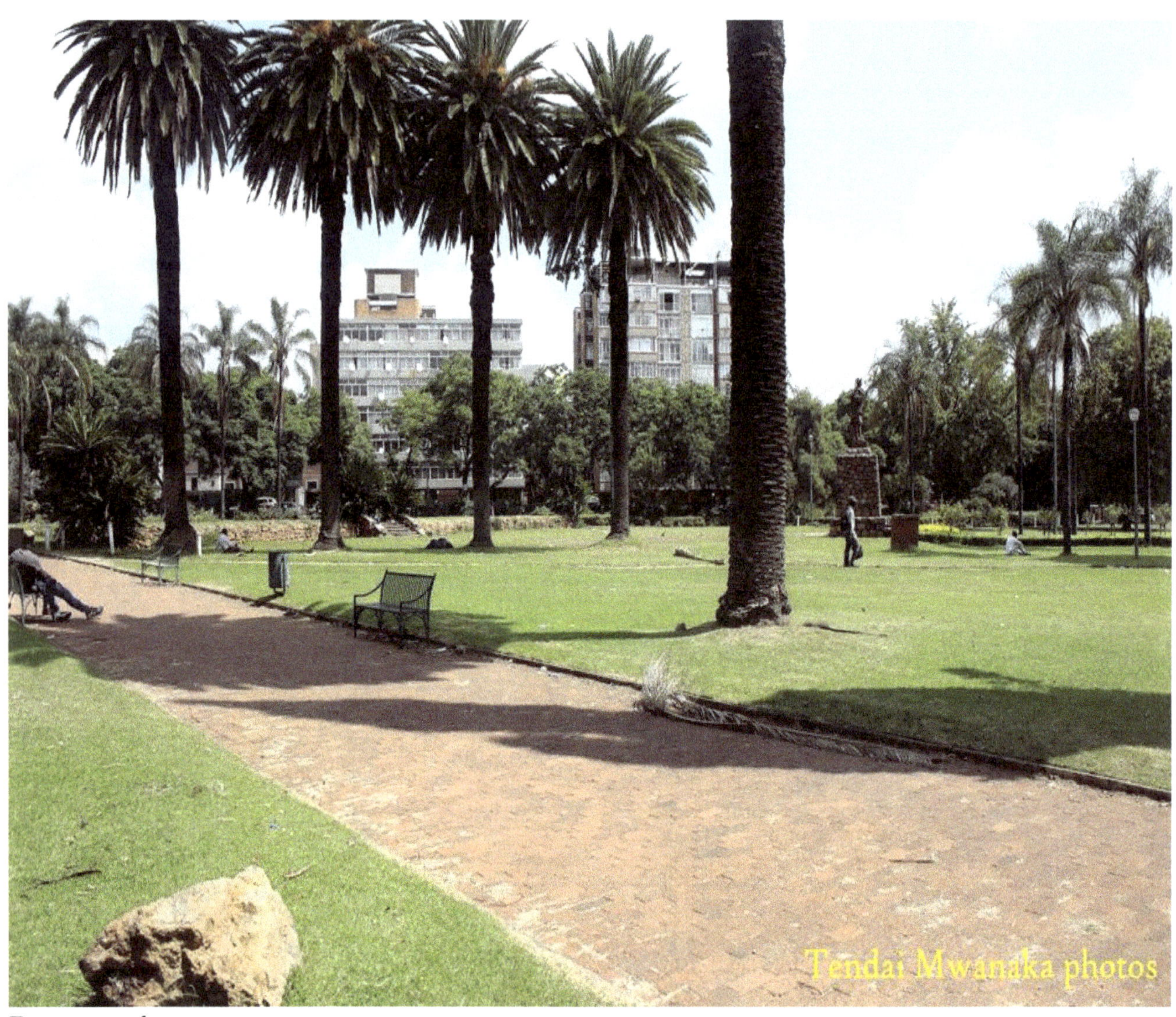

Burgers park
2022

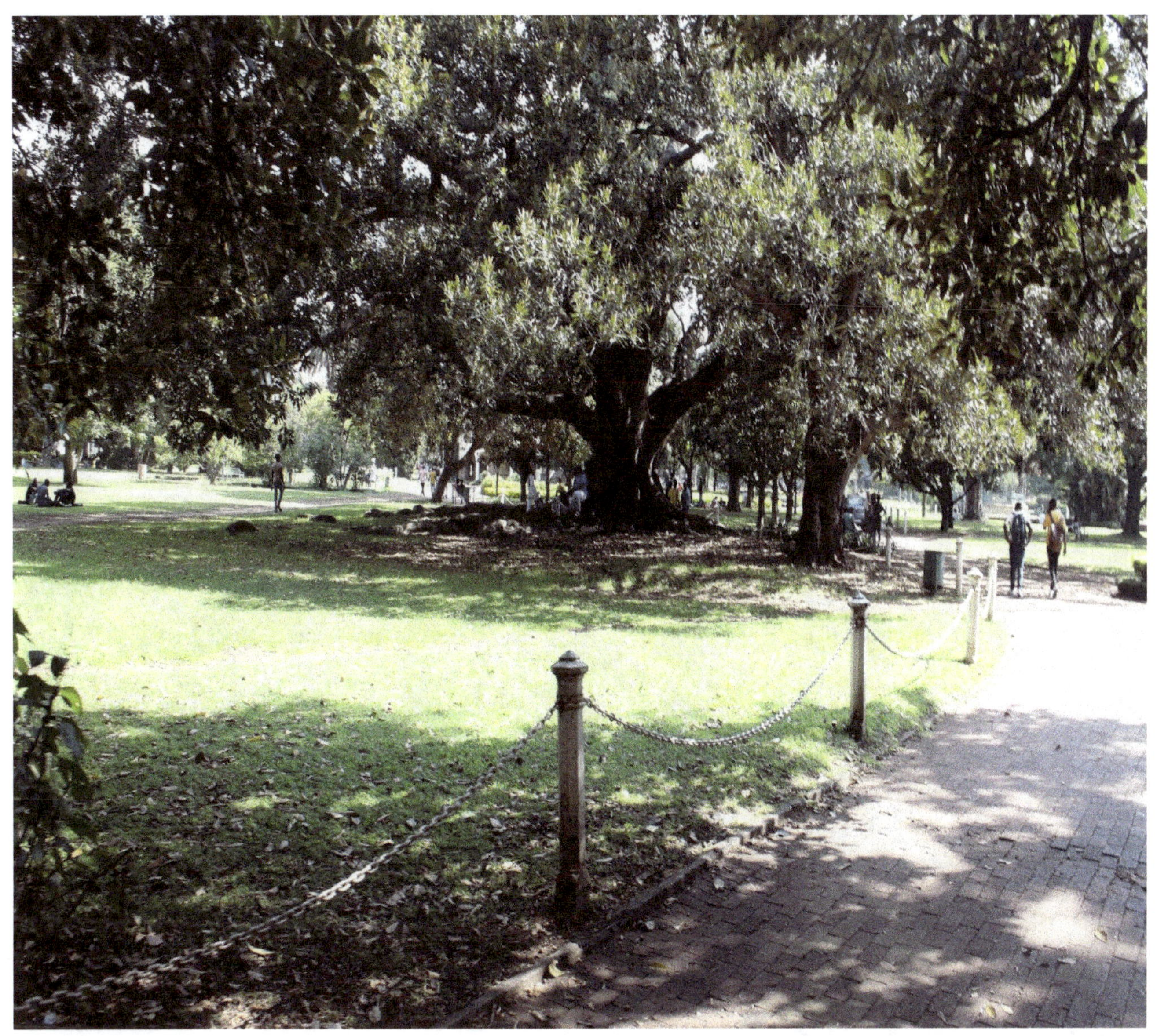

The Big shade
2022

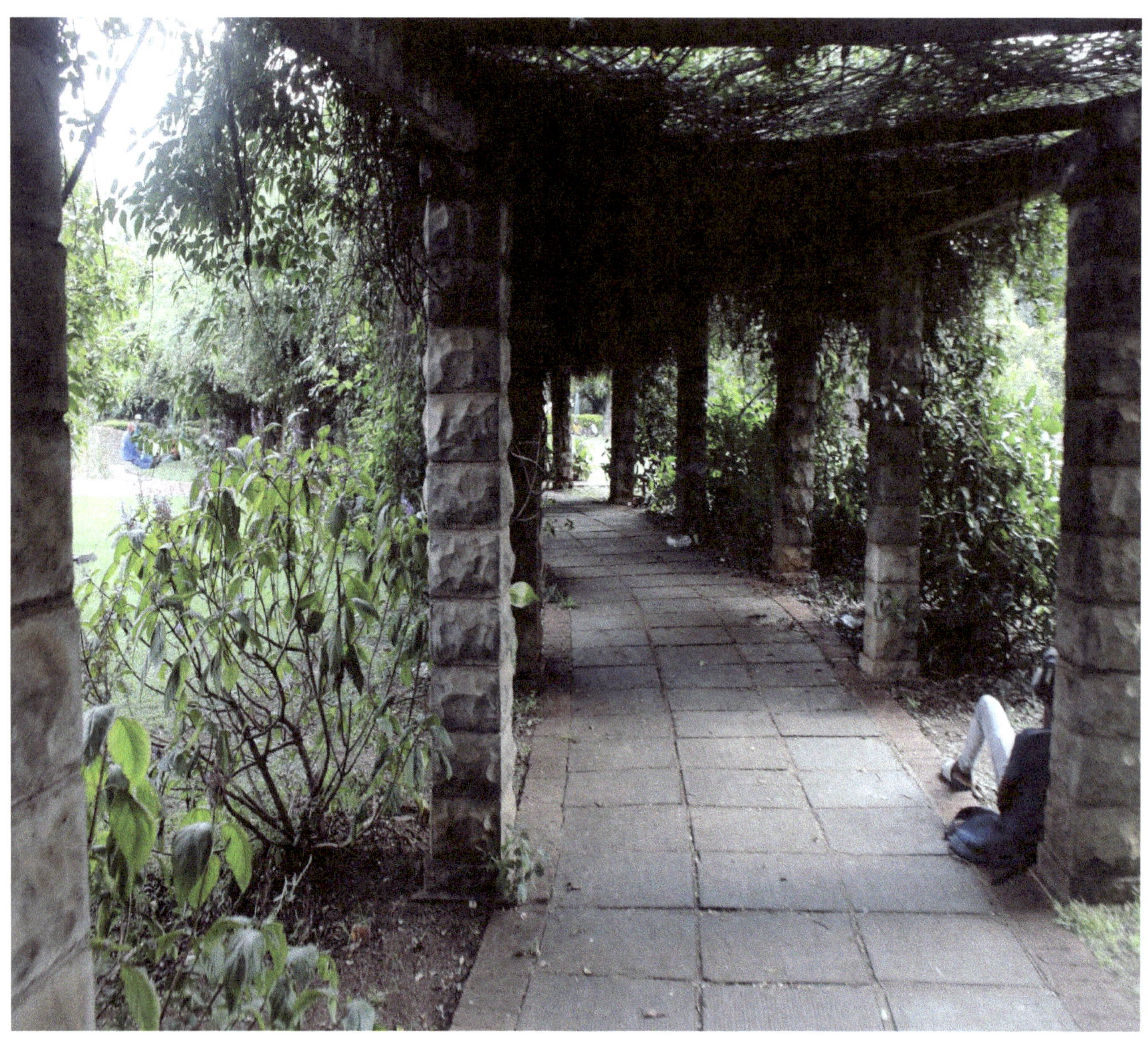

Open Cave
2022

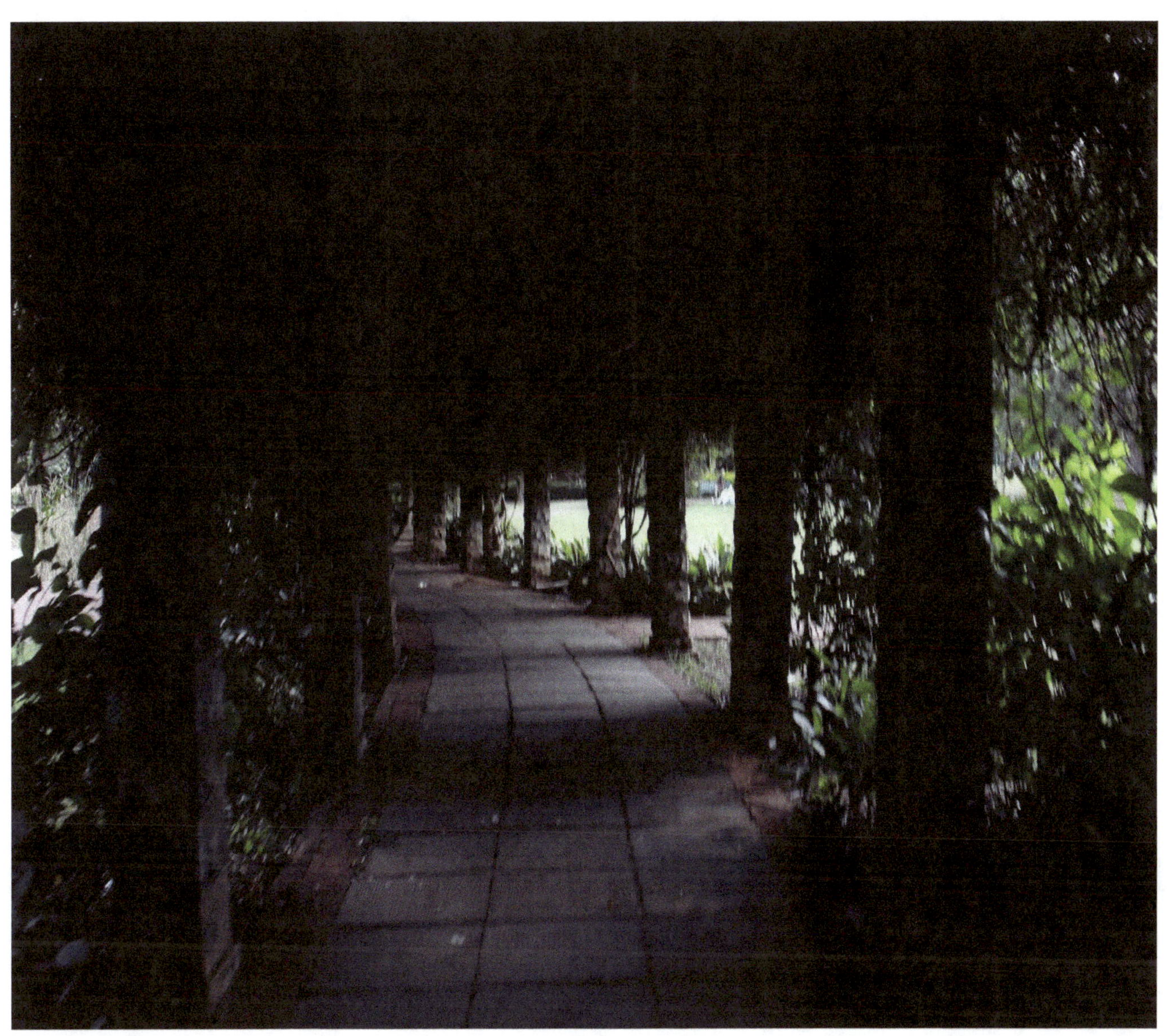

Inside the Cave
2022

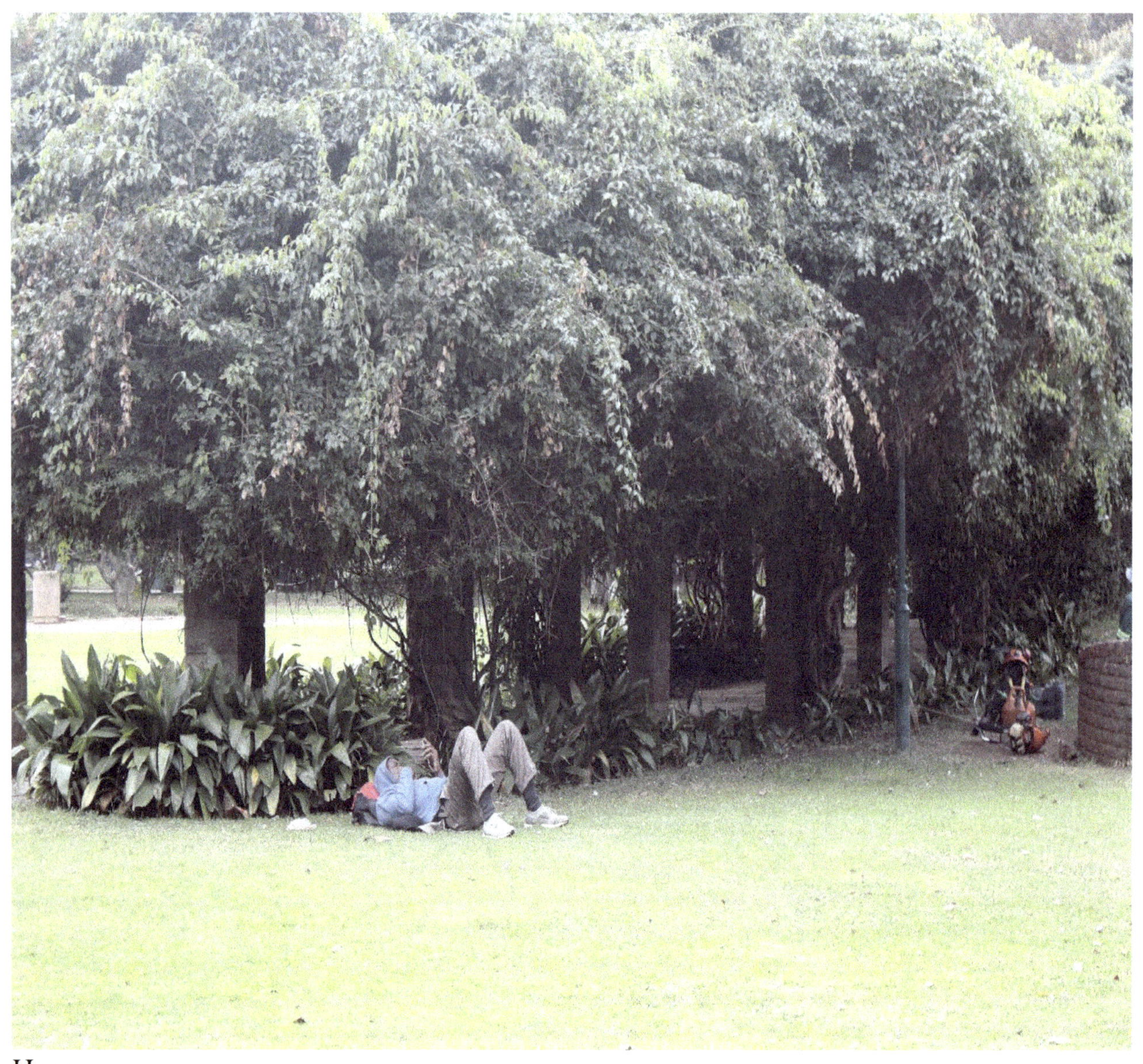

House
2022

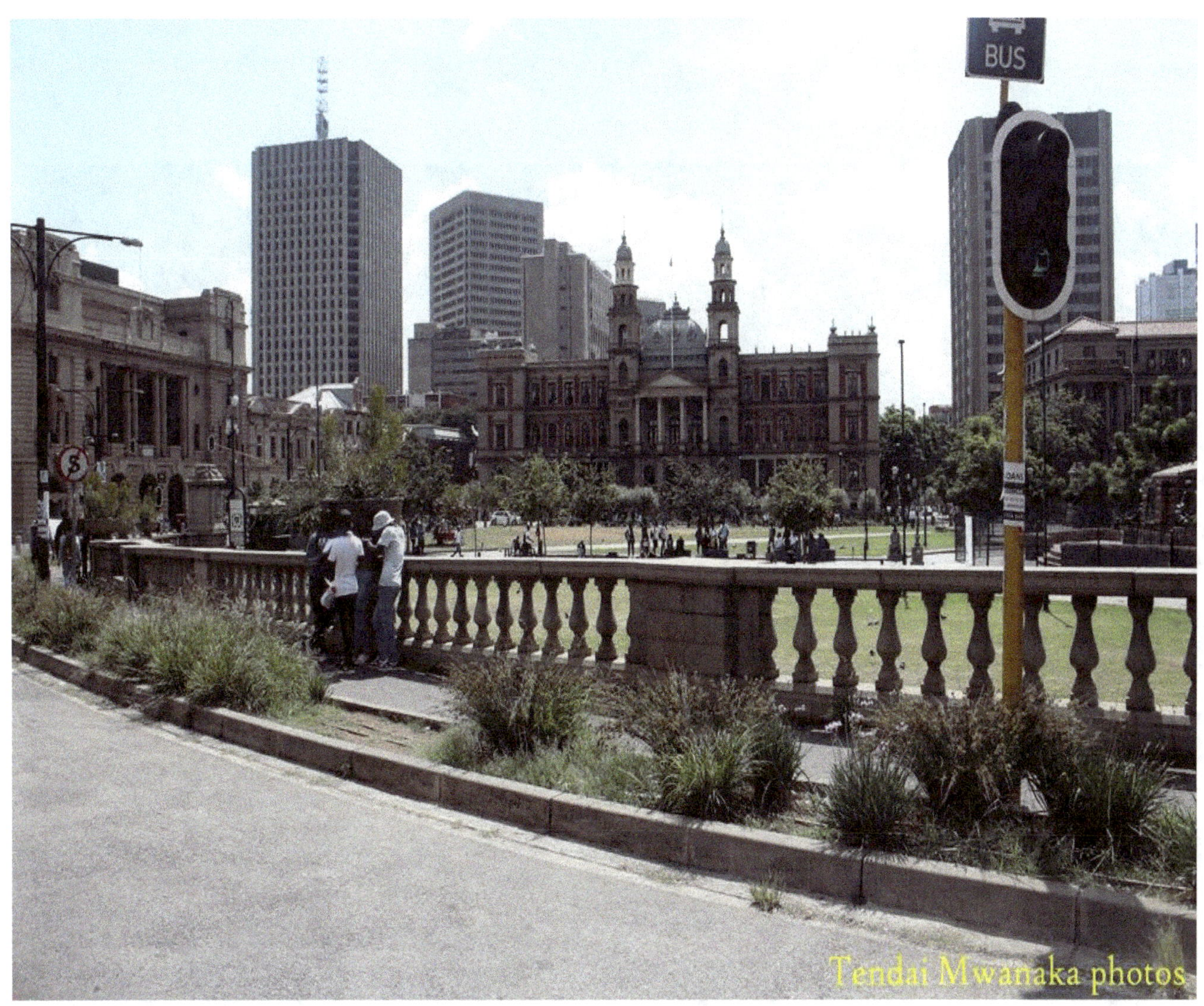

Circular Church Square
2022

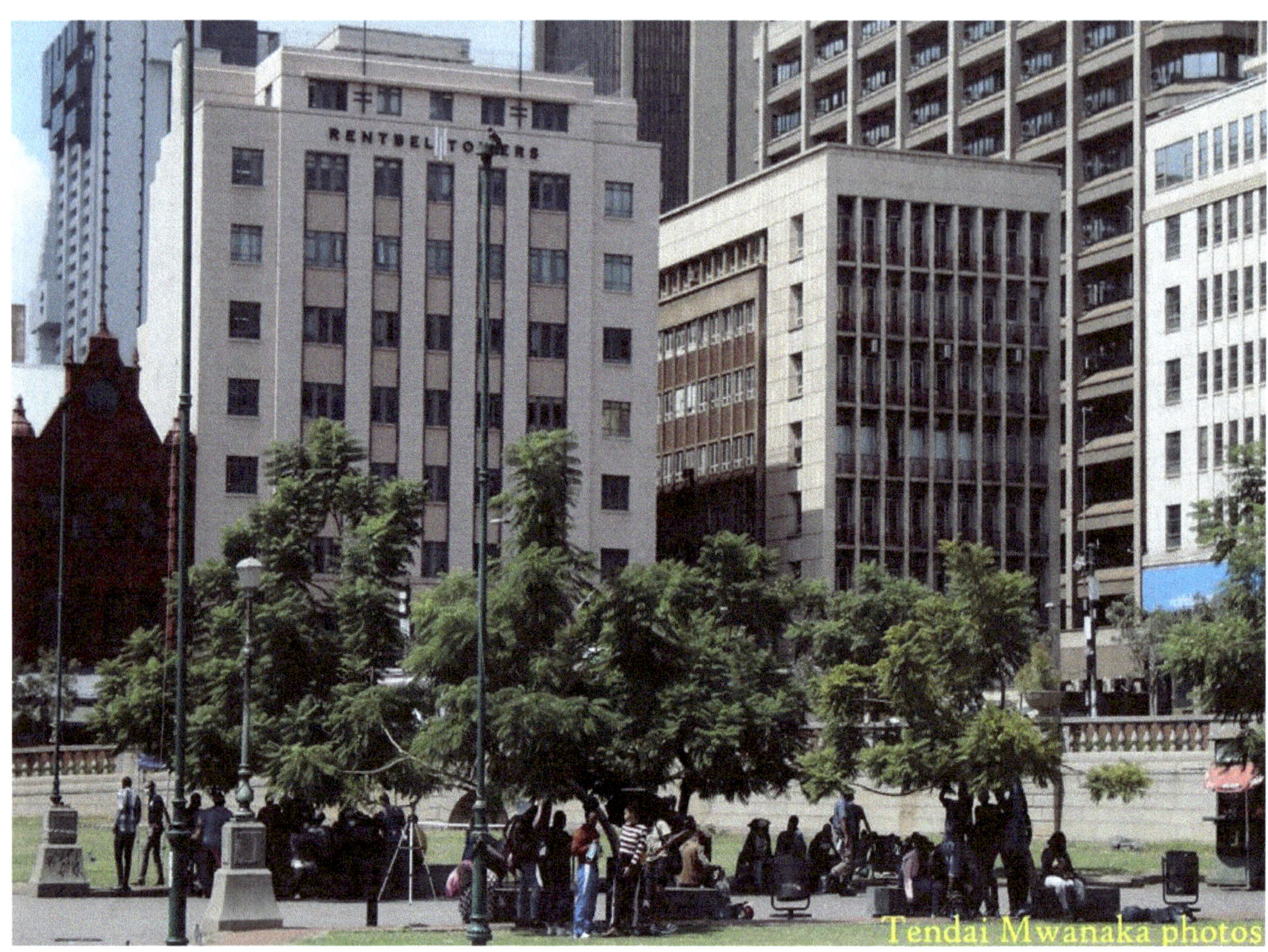

Standing under our Gods
2022

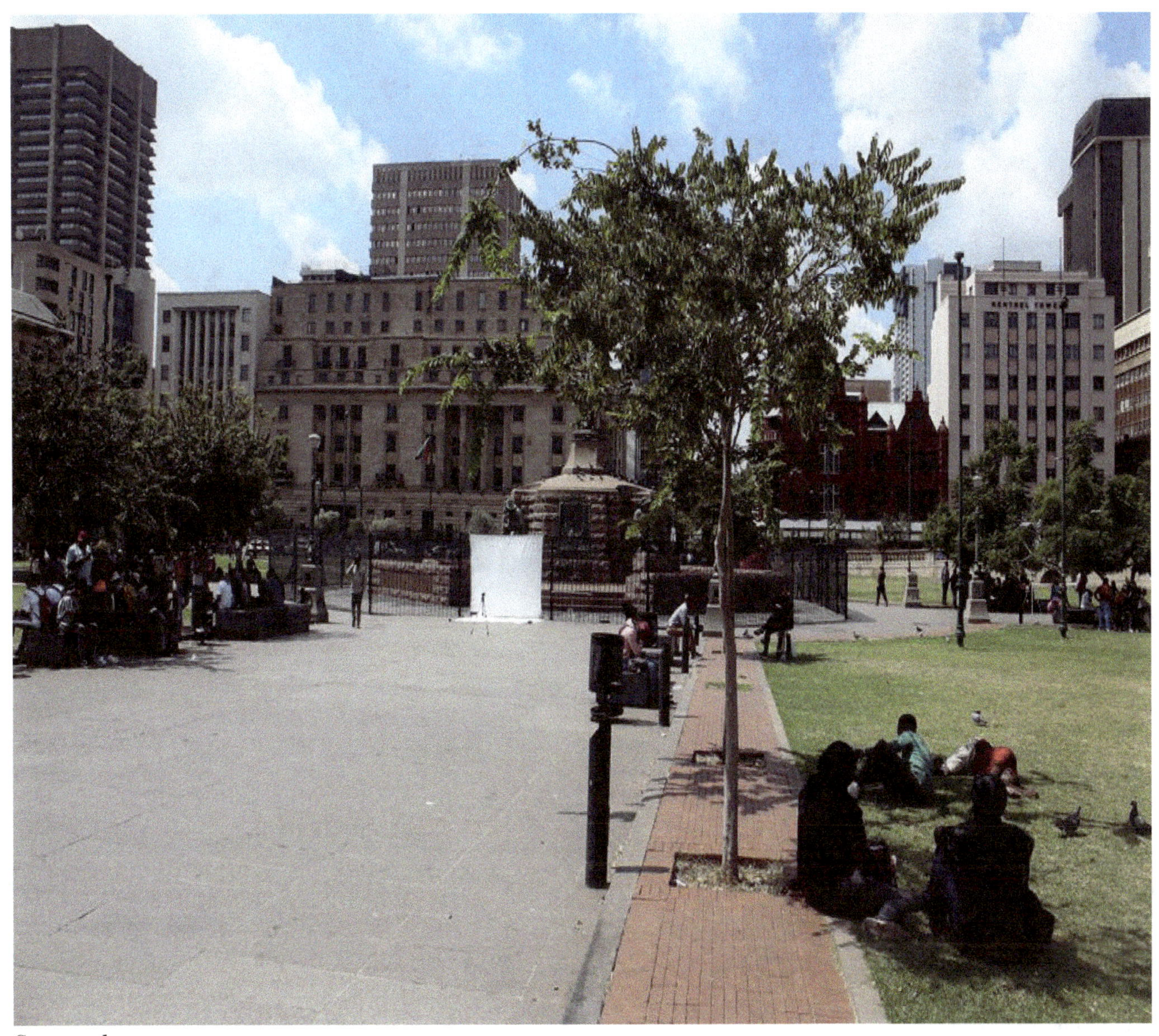

Square dreams
2022

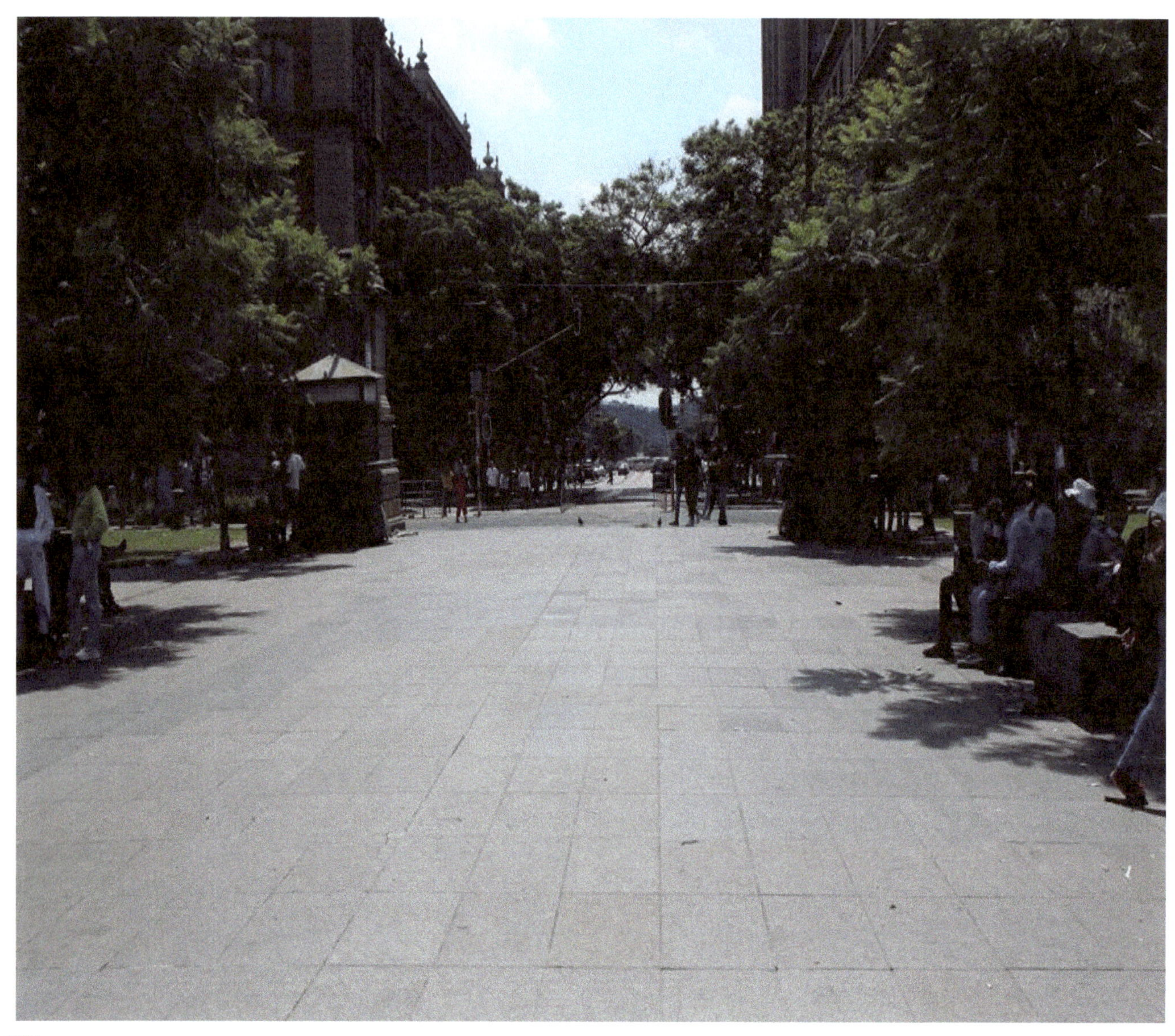

Way out
2022

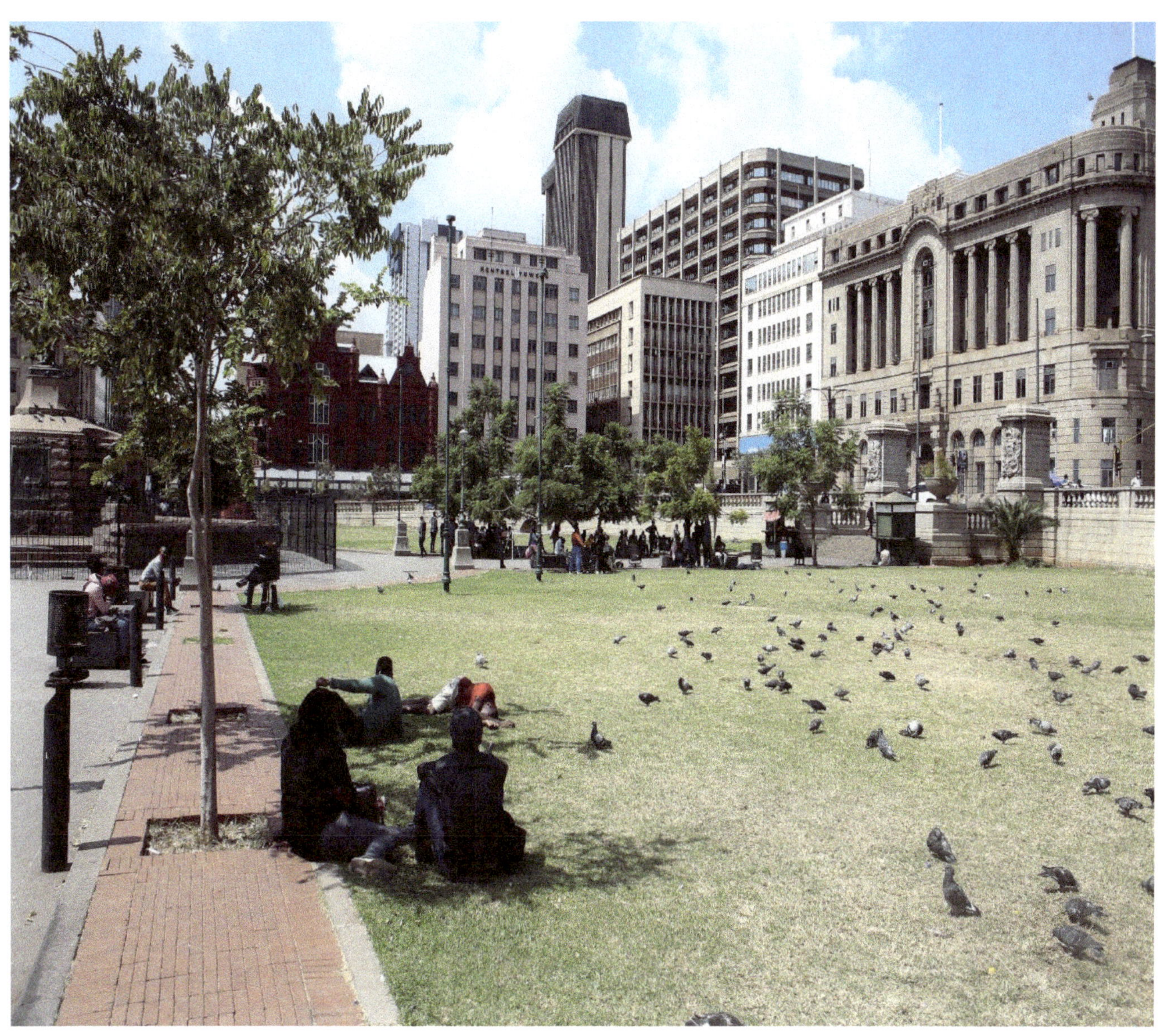

Sharing the park
2022

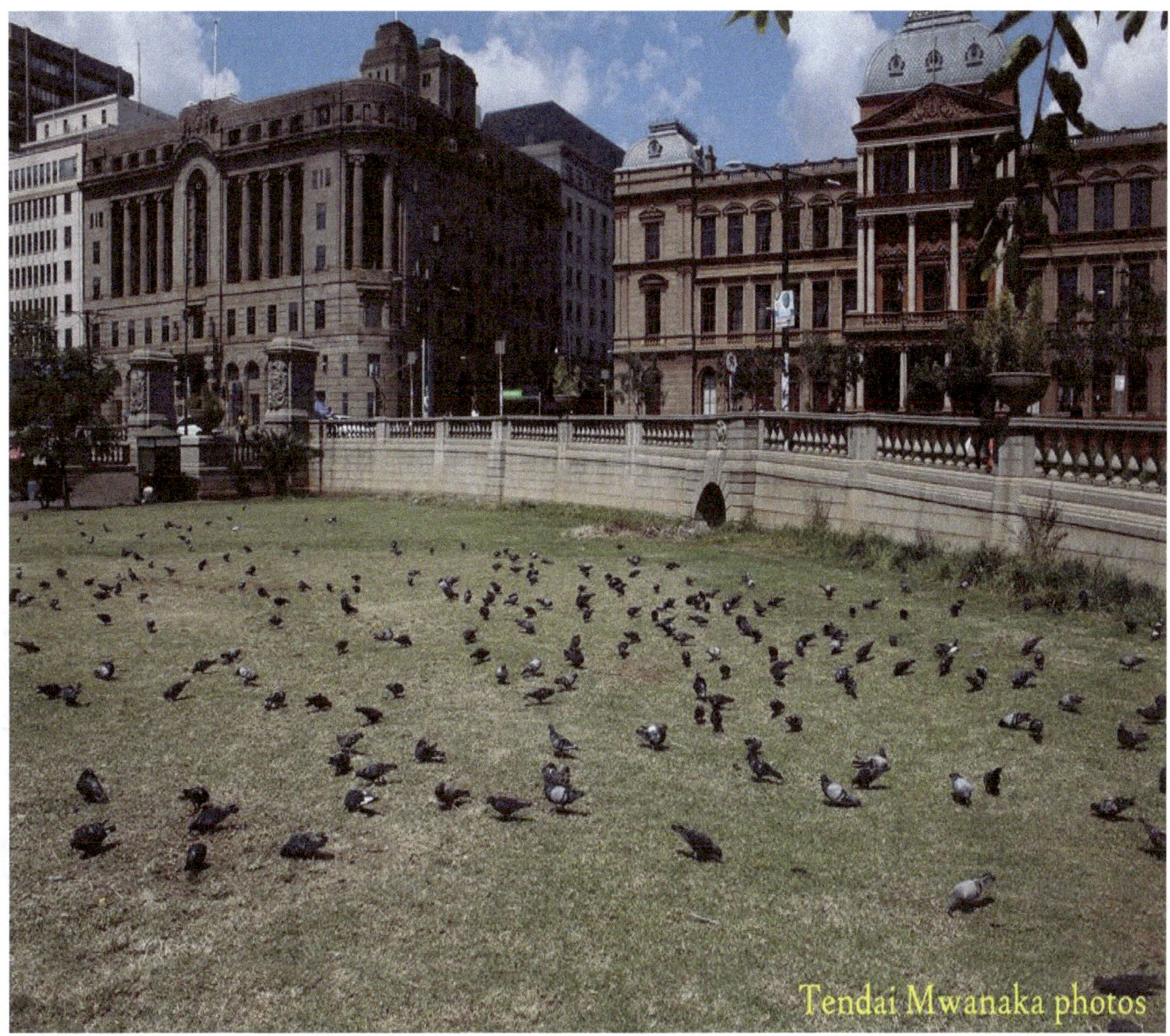

Pigeons of Pretoria
2022

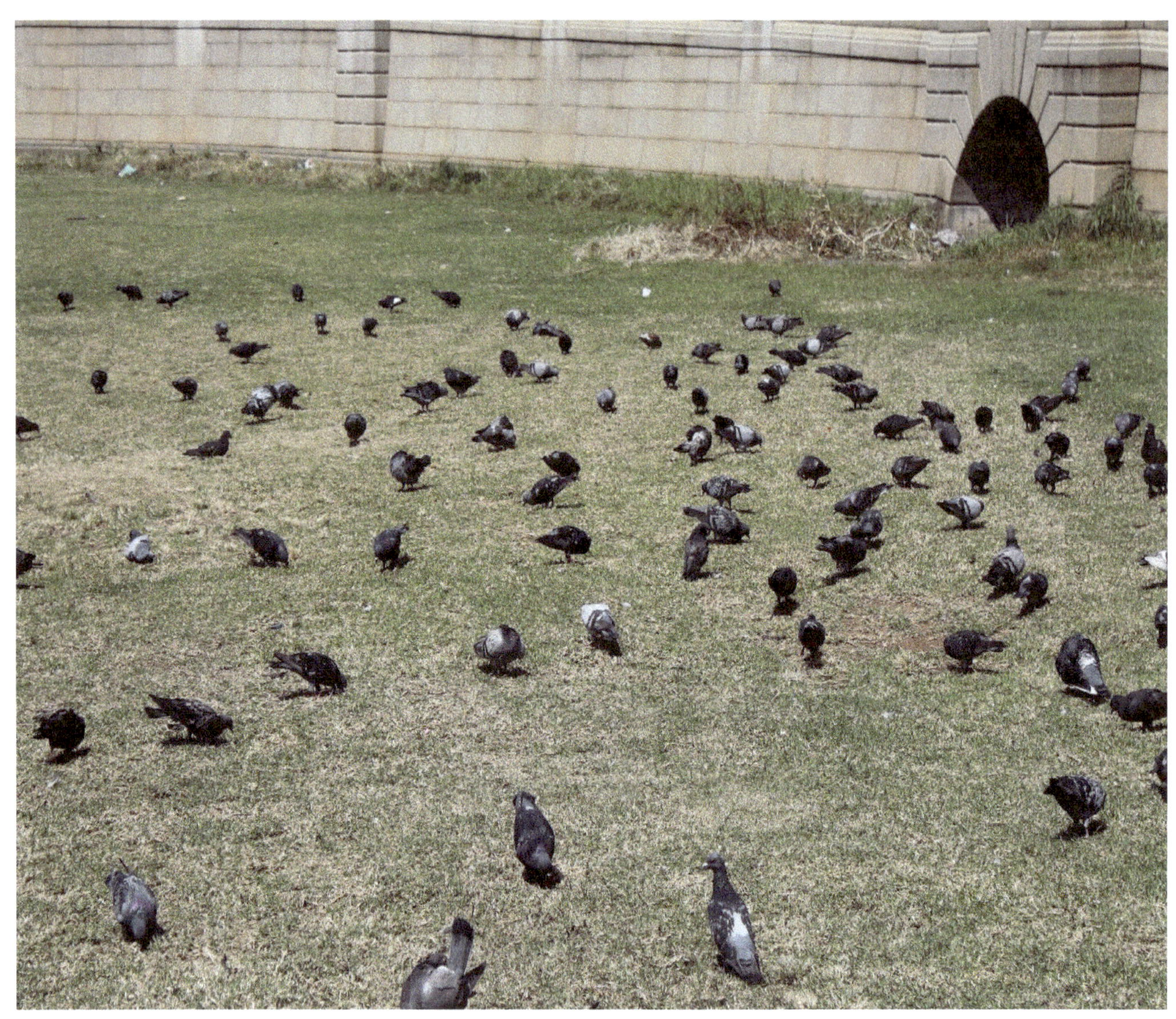

Plumage
2022

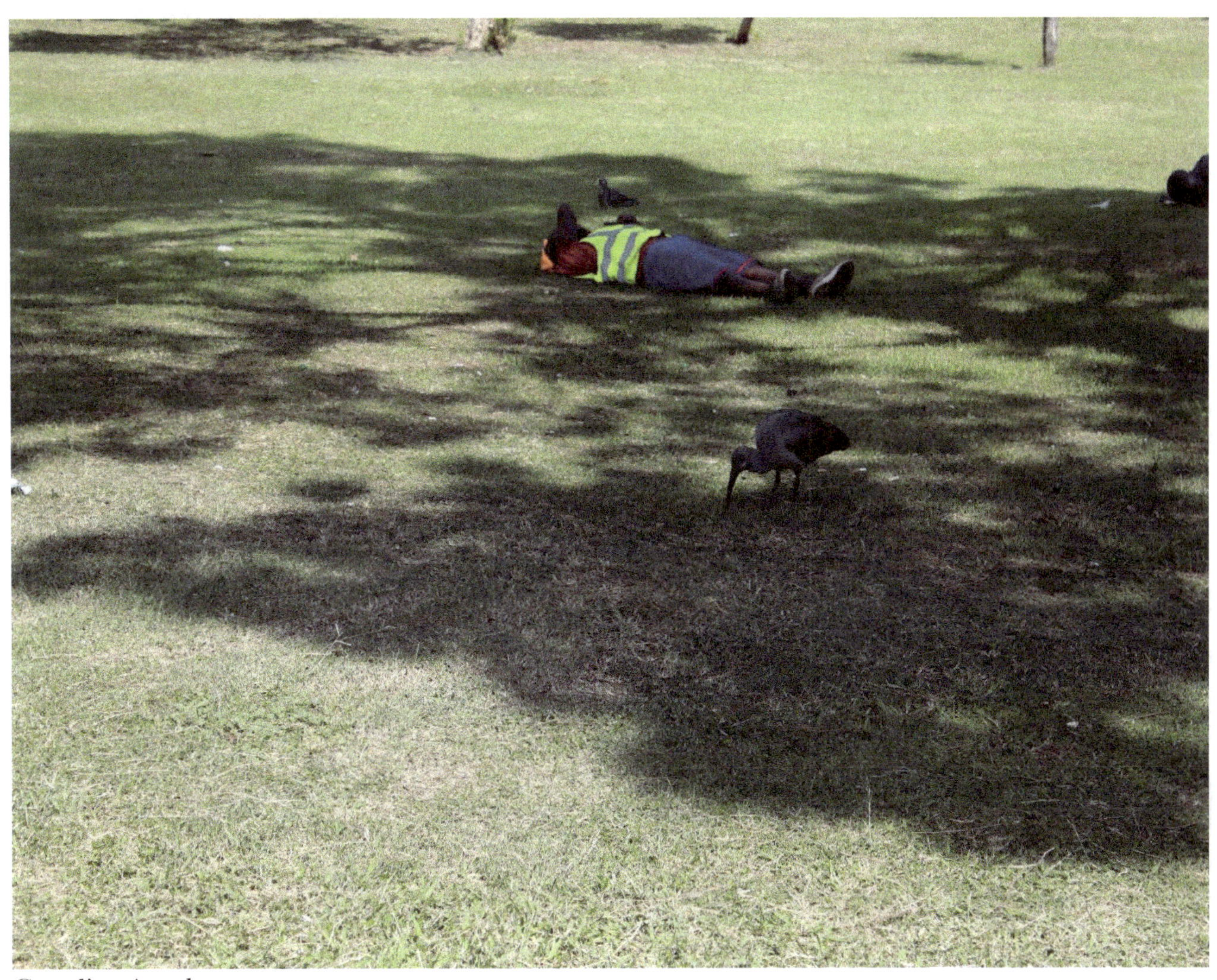

Guardian Angels
2022

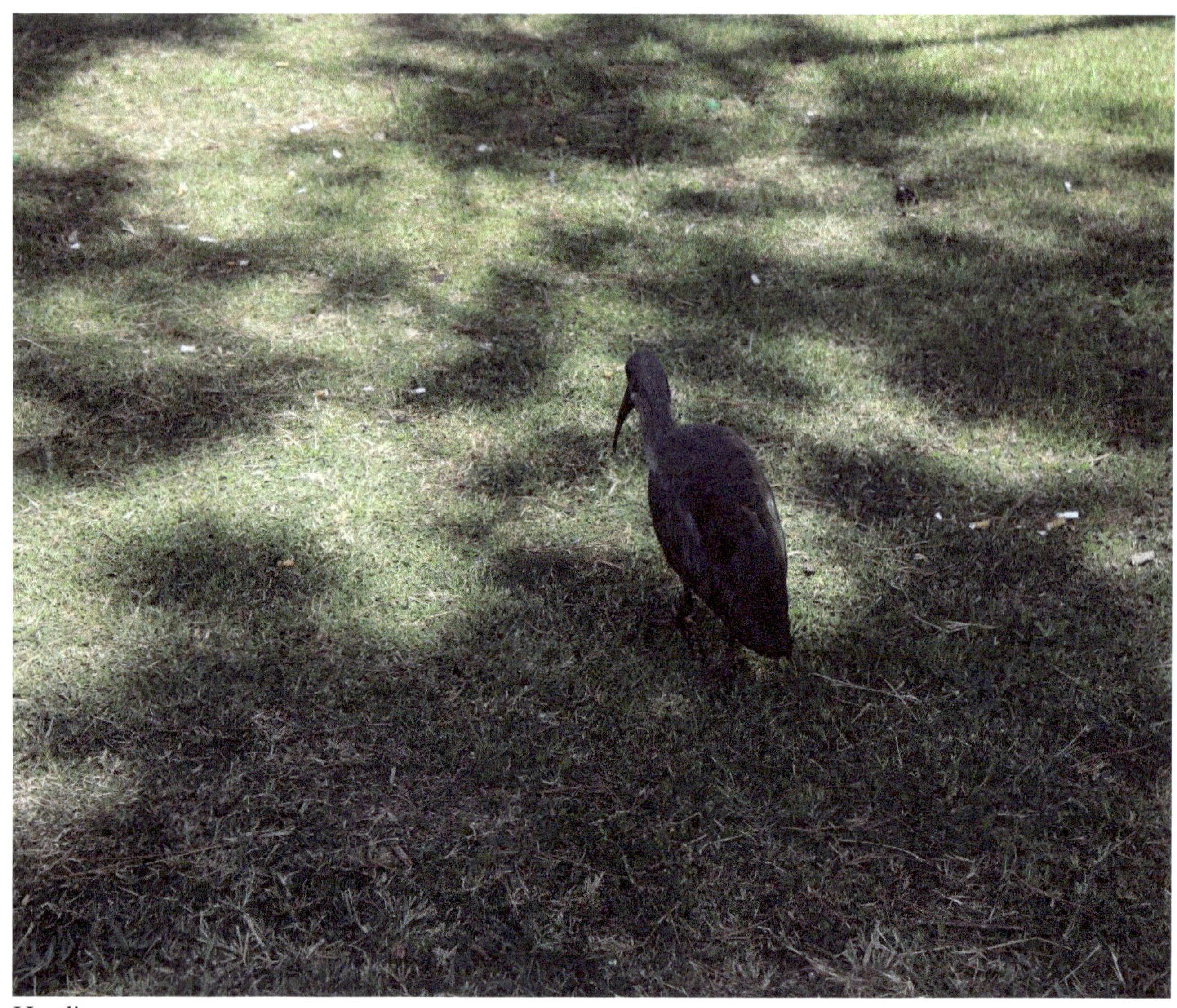

Hustling
2022

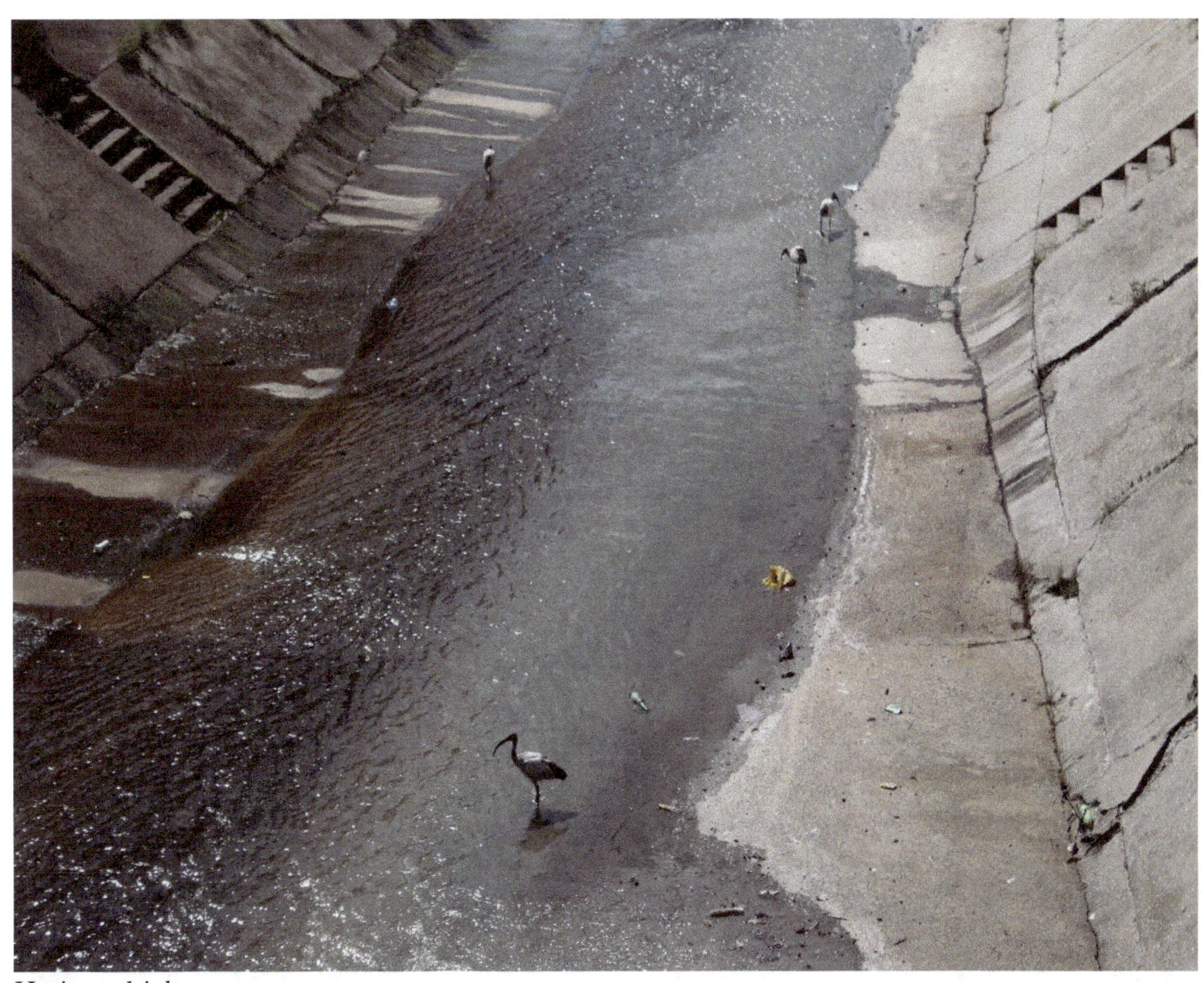

Having a drink
2022

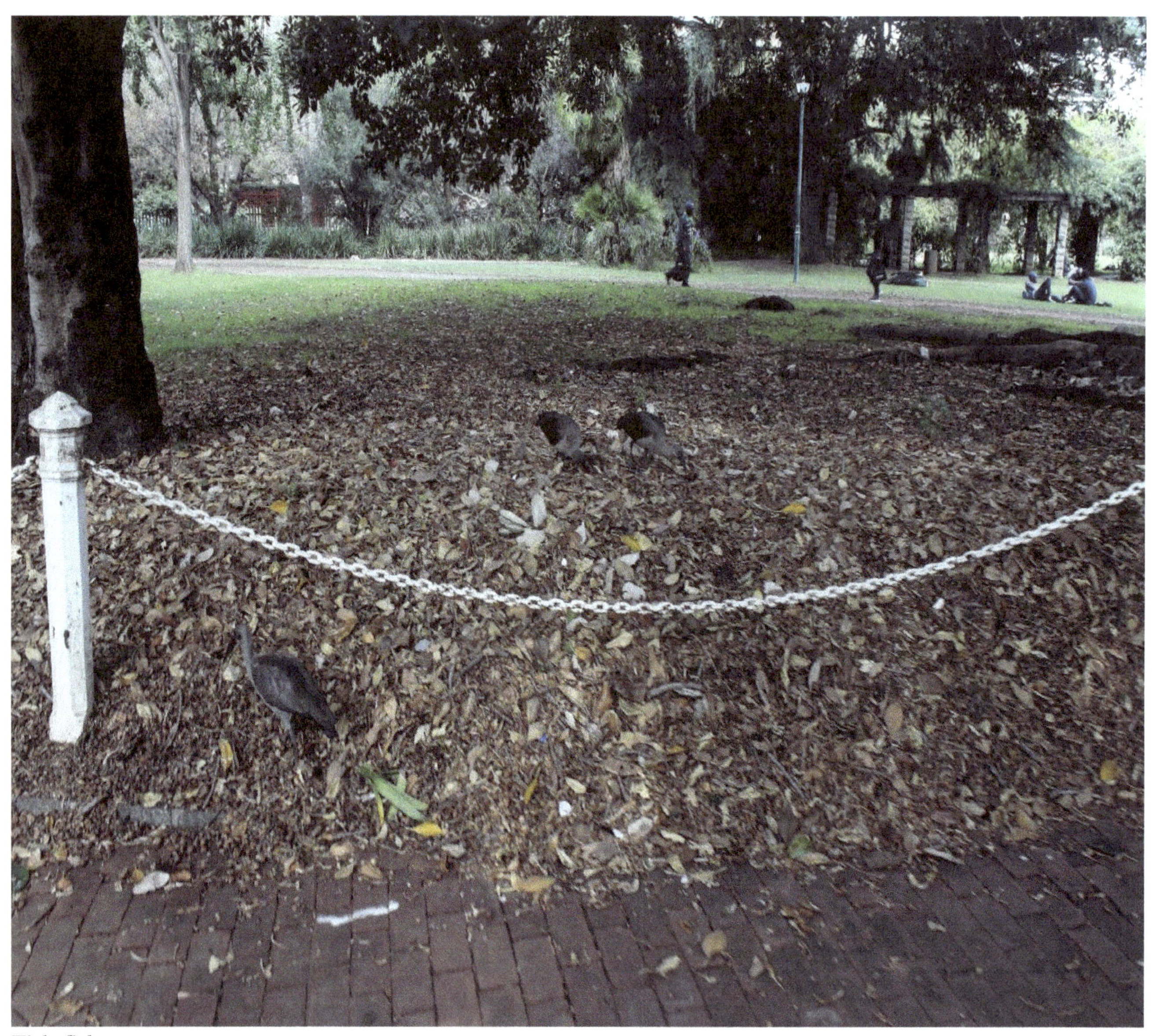

Fish fish
2022

CITY WIDE VIEWS

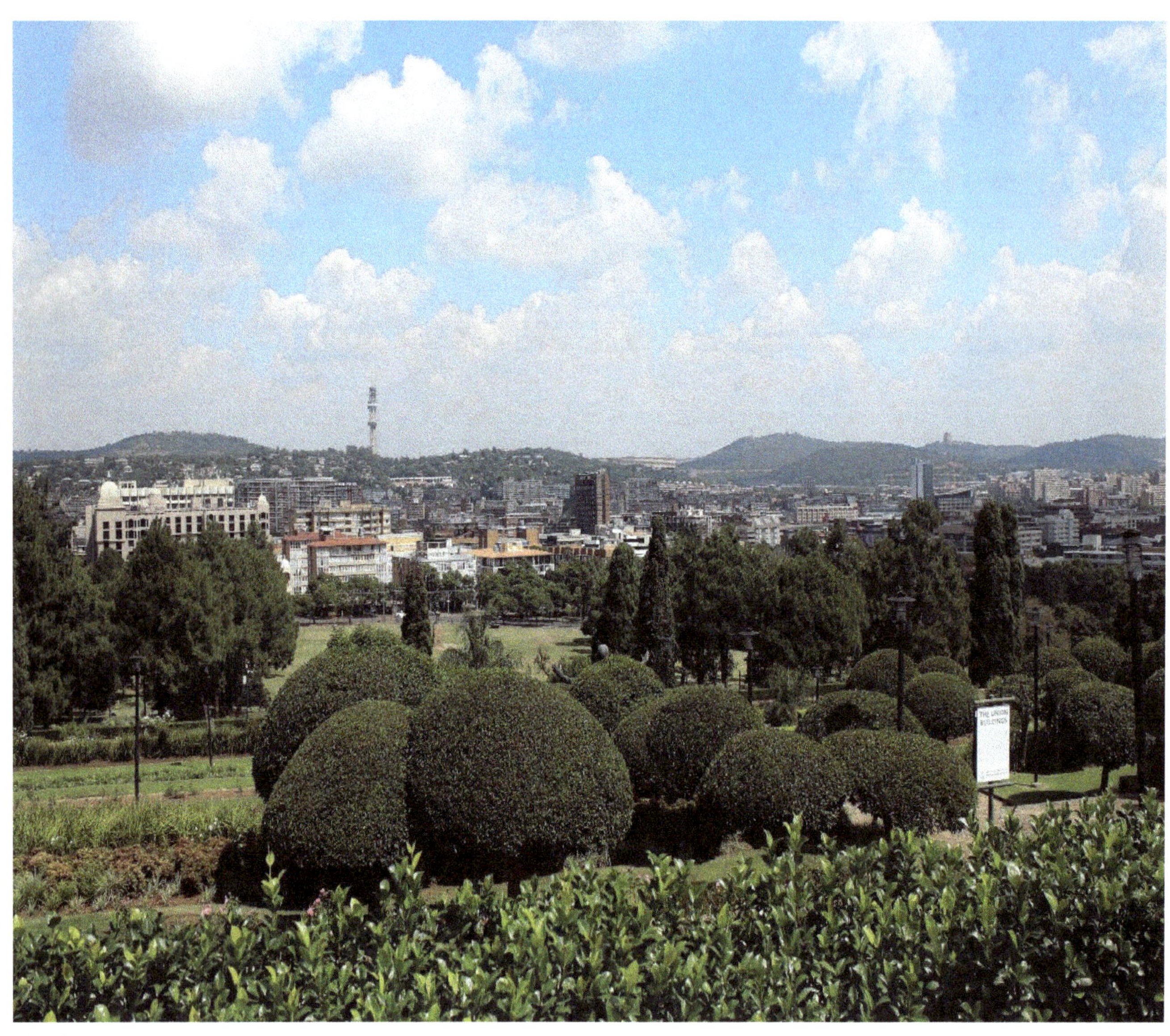

Cityview 1
2022

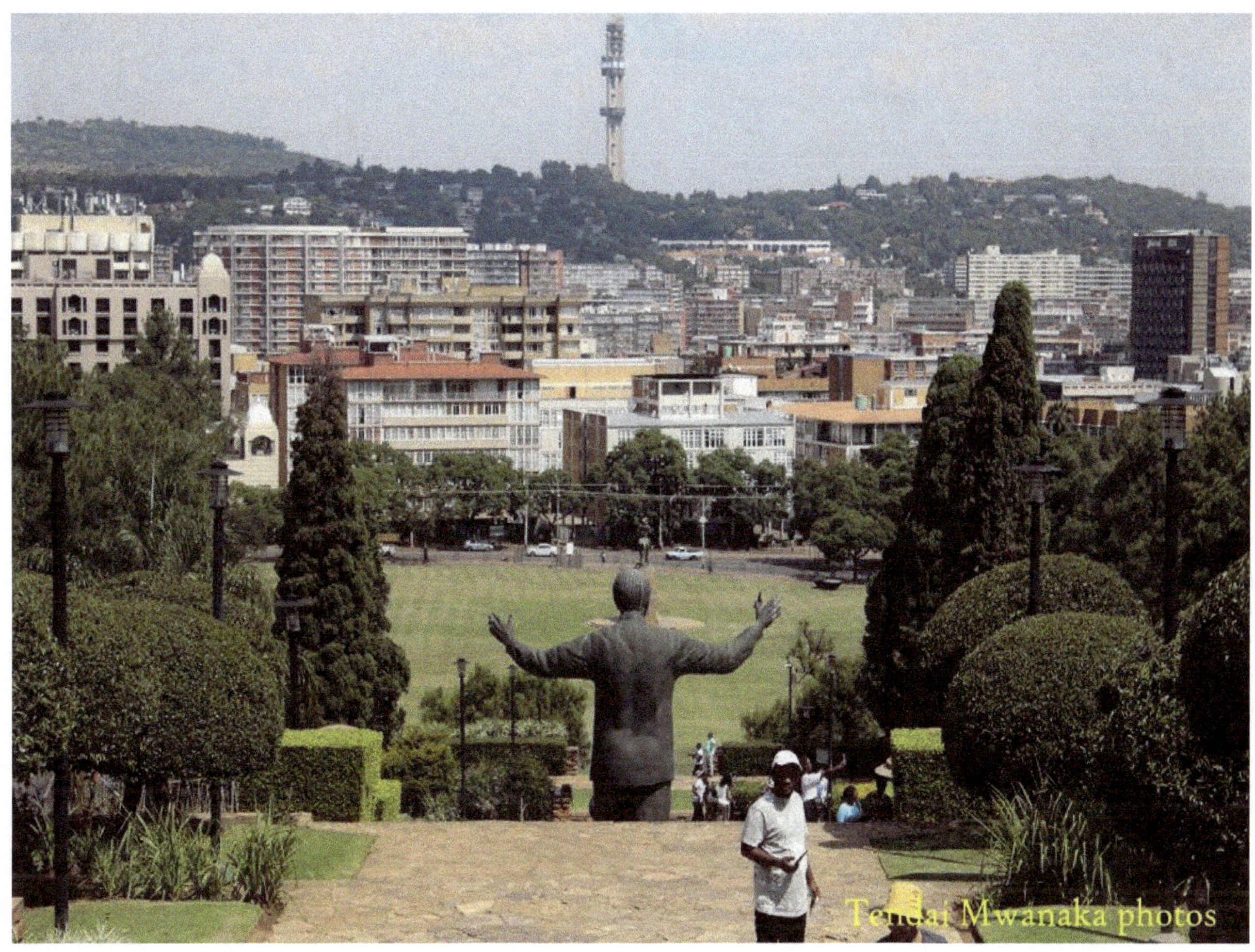

Welcome to my city
2022

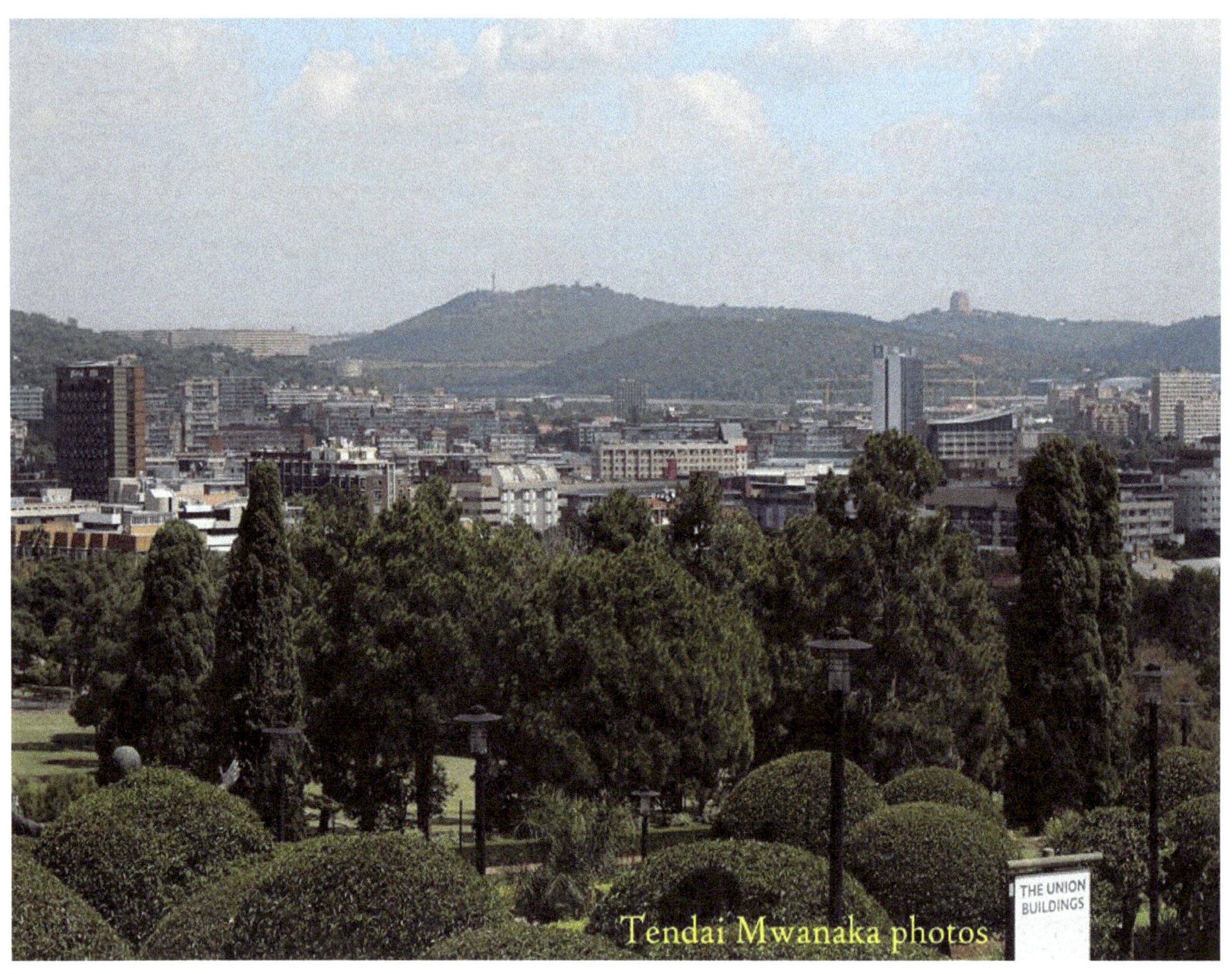

Cityview 2
2022

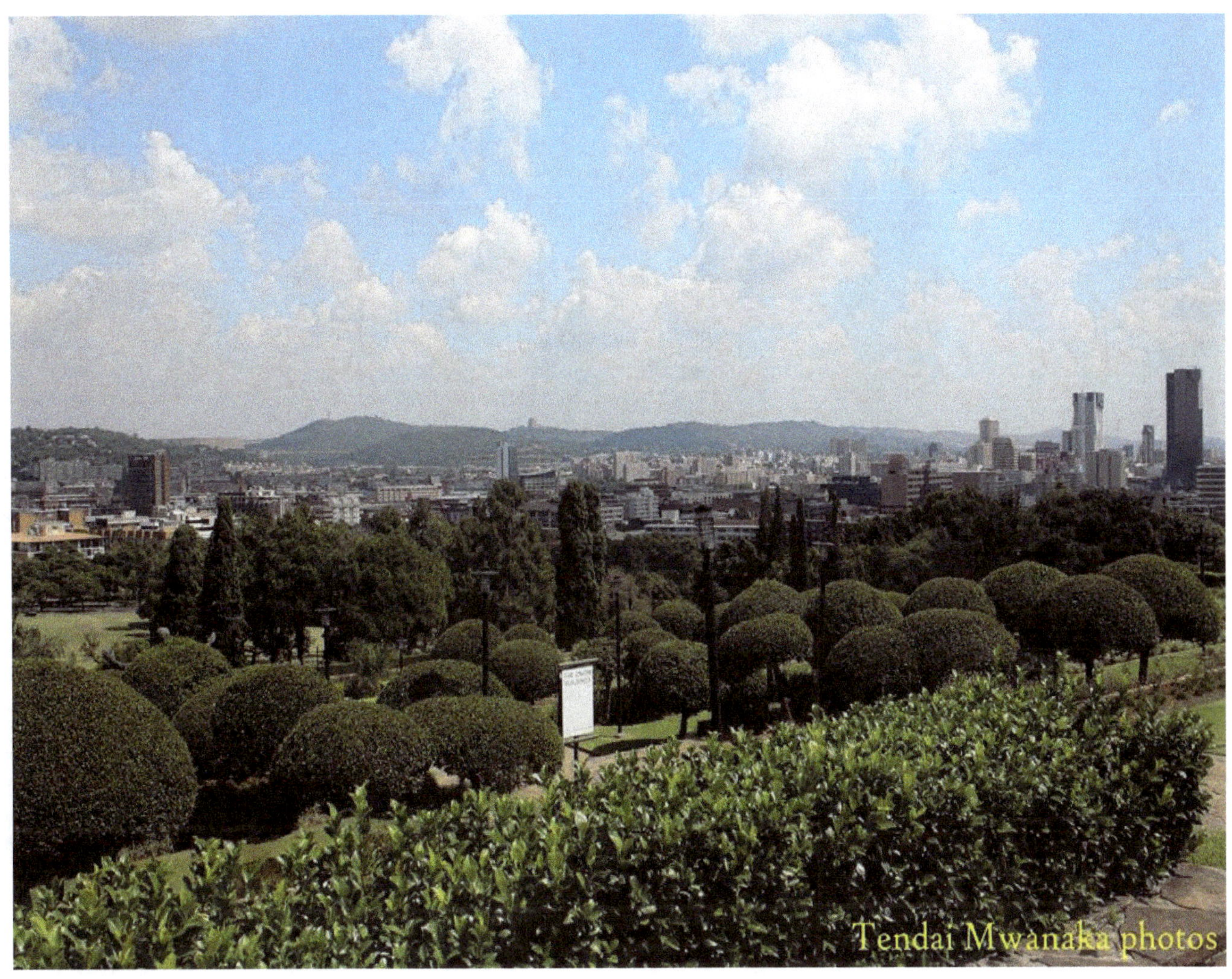

Cityview 3
2022

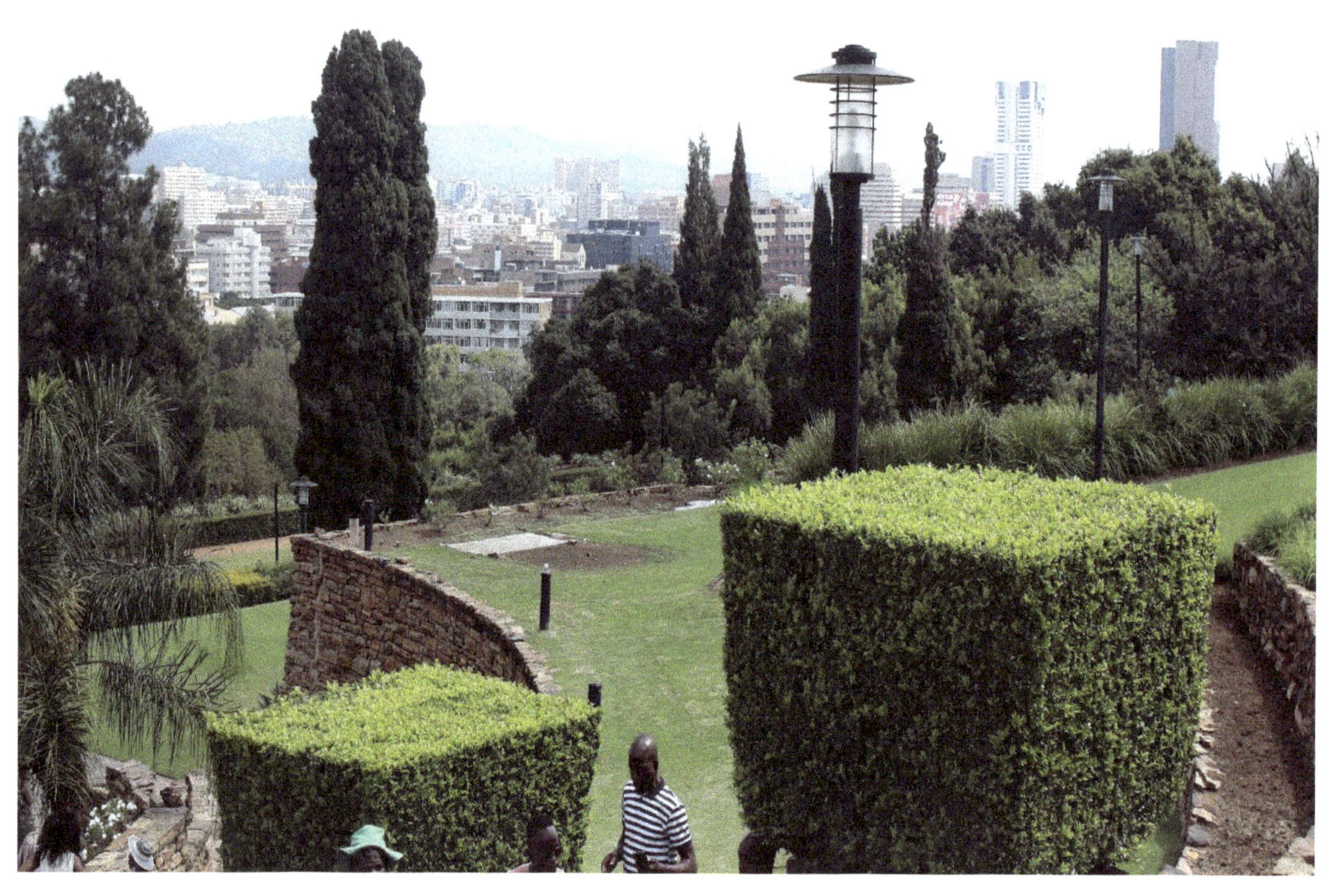

Cityview 4
2022

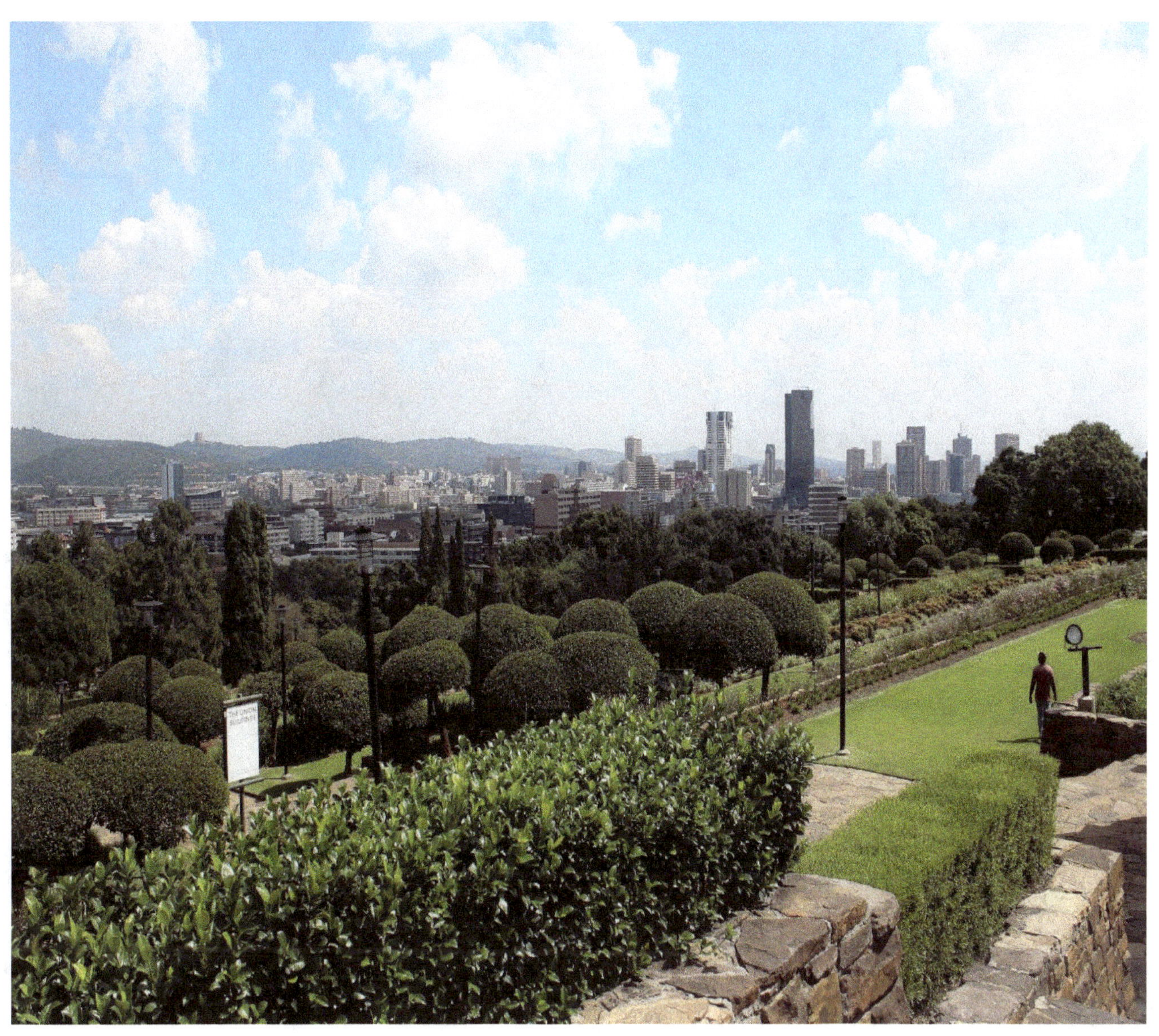

Cityview 5
2022

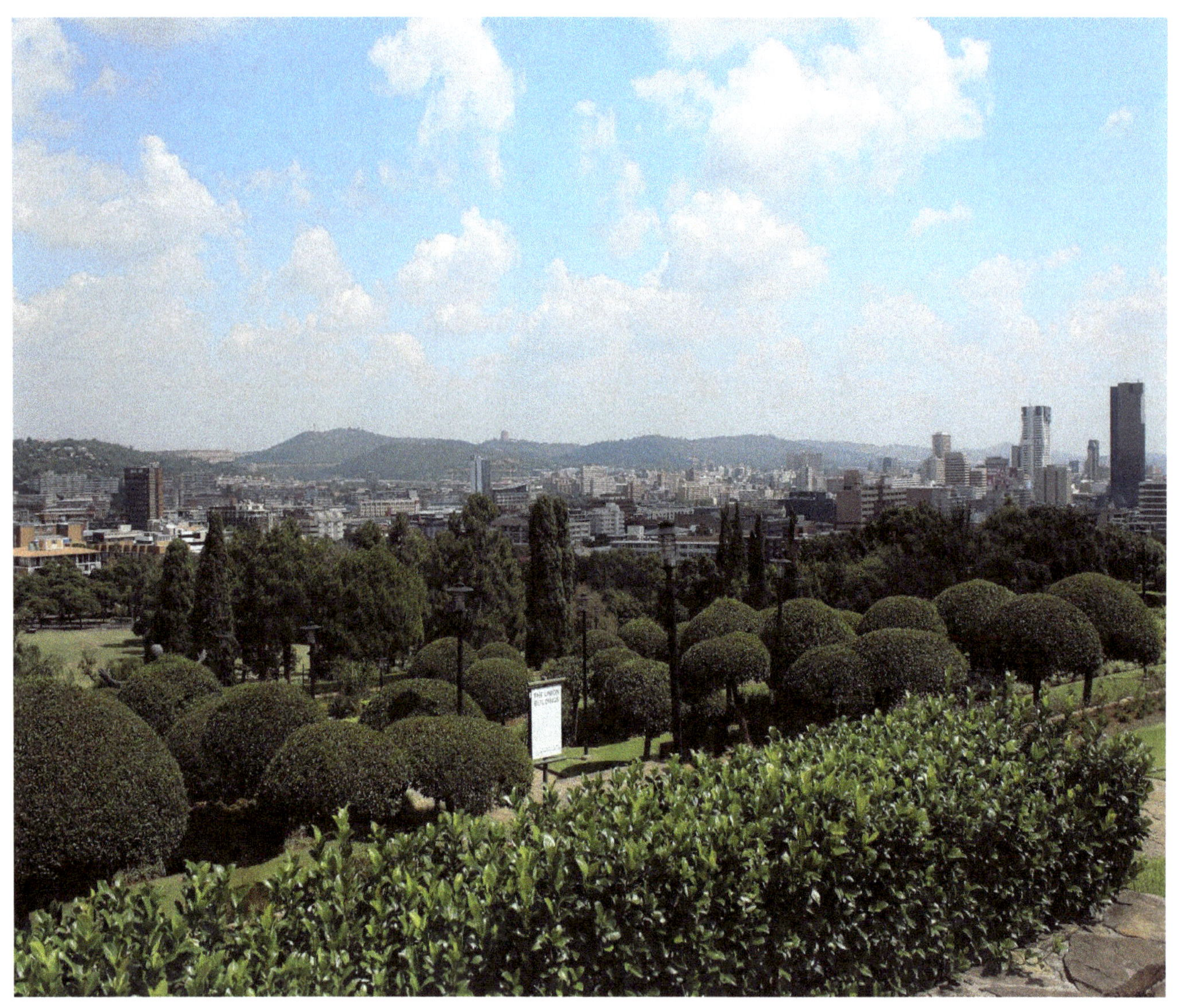

Cityview 6
2022

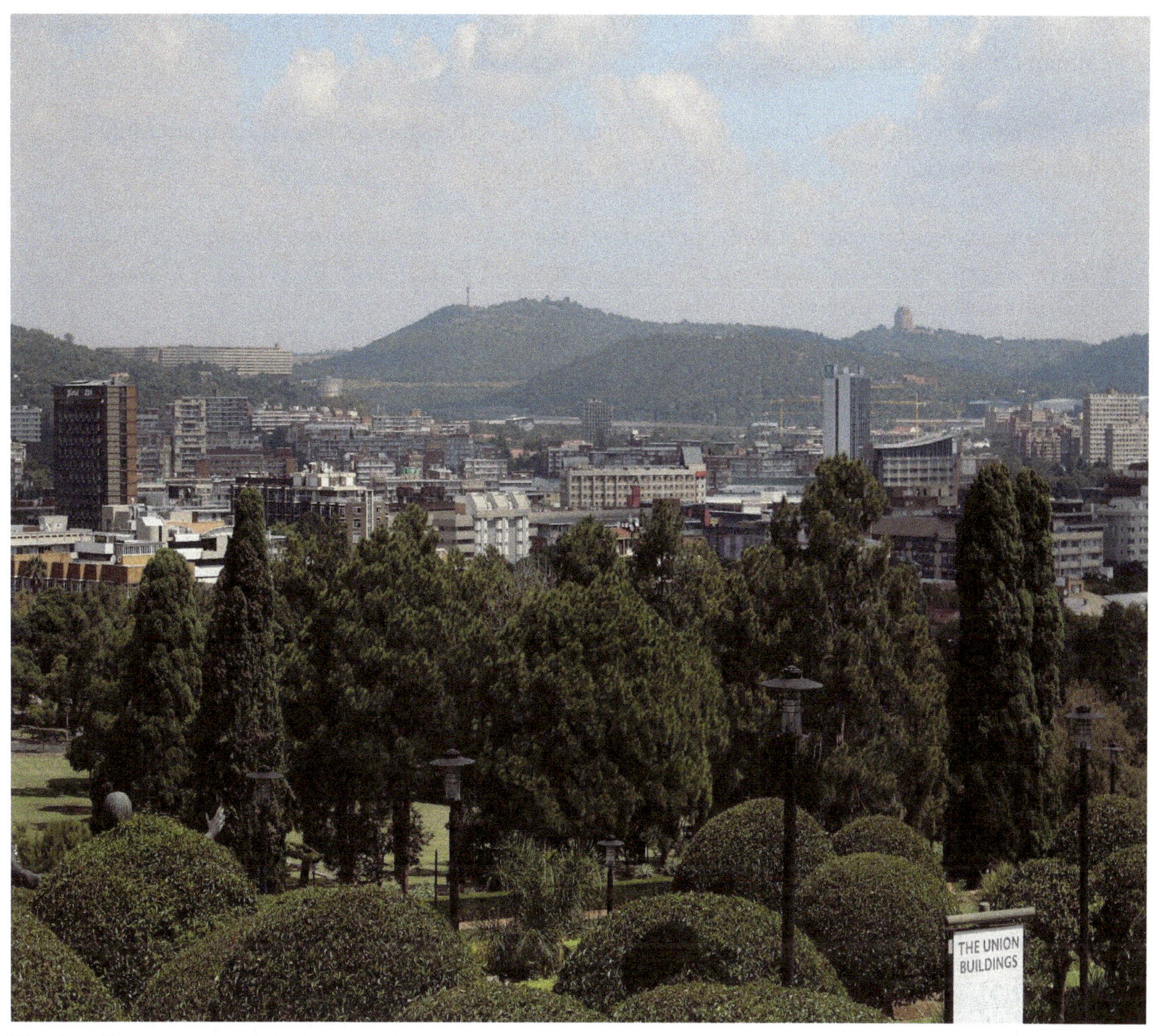

Cityview 7
2022

Mmap Multi-disciplinary Series

If you have enjoyed *Pretty Pretorialicious,* consider these other fine books in the **Mmap Multi-disciplinary Series** from *Mwanaka Media and Publishing:*

Africanization and Americanization Anthology Volume 1, Searching for Interracial, Interstitial, Intersectional and Interstates Meeting Spaces, Africa Vs North America by Tendai R Mwanaka
A Conversation..., A Contact by Tendai Rinos Mwanaka
Africa, UK and Ireland: Writing Politics and Knowledge Production Vol 1 by Tendai R Mwanaka
Writing Language, Culture and Development, Africa Vs Asia Vol 1 by Tendai R Mwanaka, Wanjohi wa Makokha and Upal Deb
Zimbolicious: An Anthology of Zimbabwean Literature and Arts, Vol 3 by Tendai Mwanaka
Drawing Without Licence by Tendai R Mwanaka
Writing Grandmothers/ Escribiendo sobre nuestras raíces: Africa Vs Latin America Vol 2 by Tendai R Mwanaka and Felix Rodriguez
Tiny Human Protection Agency by Megan Landman
Ghetto Symphony by Mandla Mavolwane
A Portrait of Defiance by Tendai Rinos Mwanaka
Nationalism: (Mis)Understanding Donald Trump's Capitalism, Racism, Global Politics, International Trade and Media Wars, Africa Vs North America Vol 2 by Tendai R Mwanaka
Ouafa and Thawra: About a Lover From Tunisia by Arturo Desimone
Zimbolicious: An Anthology of Zimbabwean Literature and Arts, Vol 4 by Tendai Mwanaka and Jabulani Mzinyathi
Chitungwiza Mushamukuru Anthology by Tendai Rinos Mwanaka
The Day and the Dweller: A Study of the Emerald Tablets by Jonathan Thompson
Zimbolicious: An Anthology of Zimbabwean Literature and Arts, Vol 5 by Tendai Mwanaka
Robotics Anthology, Africa vs Asia Vol 2 by Tendai Rinos Mwanaka
Shaping Up by Tendai Rinos Mwanaka
Zimbolicious Anthology Vol 6: An Anthology of Zimbabwean Literature and Arts by Tendai Rinos Mwanaka and Chenjerai Mhondera

Registers of Loss: PhotoTalking to the Baobab Trees of Nyatate by Tendai Rinos Mwanaka
The Trick is to Keep Breathing: Covid 19 Stories From African and North American Writers, vol 3 by Tendai Rinos Mwanaka
Fixing Earth: An Anthology of Ireland, UK and Africa Writers, Vol 2 by Tendai Rinos Mwanaka
Zimbolicious: An Anthology of Zimbabwean Literature and Arts, Vol 7 Tendai Rinos Mwanaka and Tanaka Chidora
Writing Woman Anthology: Personal Essays and Short stories, An Anthology of African and Asian Writers, Vol 3 by Tendai Rinos Mwanaka, Abigail George, Sue Zhu and Monalisa Jena
Writing Woman Anthology: Drama and Scholarly Essays, An Anthology of African and Asian Writers, Vol 3 by Tendai Rinos Mwanaka, Abigail George, Sue Zhu and Monalisa Jena
WRITING WOMAN ANTHOLOGY: Poetry and Visual art by Tendai Rinos Mwanaka, Abigail George, Sue Zhu and Monalisa Jena
Zimbolicious: An Anthology of Zimbabwean Literature and Arts, Vol 8 by Tendai Rinos Mwanaka and Matthew Kunashe Chikono
Of poets, gods, ghosts. Irritants and storytellers by Tendai Rinos Mwanaka
The Aporia of Unnamed Things by Tendai Rinos Mwanaka
Men: An Anthology of African and Latin American writers vol 3 by Tendai Rinos Mwanaka and Ingrid Bringas
Glyphs of Love by Tendai Rinos Mwanaka
MEN: An International Anthology of African and Latin American Writers Vol 3 by Tendai Rinos Mwanaka and Ingrid Bringas
https://facebook.com/MwanakaMediaAndPublishing/

www.ingramcontent.com/pod-product-compliance
Lightning Source LLC
LaVergne TN
LVHW081253100826
845148LV00009B/1210

9781779340405